SPIRITUALITY FROM THE DESERT

*Retreat
at Beni-Abbès*

SPIRITUALITY FROM THE DESERT

Retreat at Beni-Abbès

RENÉ VOILLAUME

*translated by
Alan Neame*

Our Sunday Visitor, Inc.
Noll Plaza, Huntington, Indiana 46750

Nihil Obstat:
Rev. Lawrence Gollner
Censor Librorum

Imprimatur:
+Leo A. Pursley, D.D.
Bishop of Fort Wayne-South Bend
November 21, 1975

First published in Great Britain in 1975
by Darton, Longman and Todd, Ltd.

This translation ©Darton, Longman and Todd, Ltd., 1975
Originally published as Retraite à Beni-Abbès by Editions du Cerf, Paris

This edition published by arrangement with Darton, Longman and Todd,
Ltd., London

ISBN: 0-87973-798-0
Library of Congress Catalog Card number: 75-37438

Cover Design by Eric Nesheim

Published, printed and bound in the U.S.A. by
Our Sunday Visitor, Inc.
Noll Plaza
Huntington, Indiana 46750

248.894

798

Translator's Note

These talks represent a course lasting for upwards of two weeks. Almost all of them are too long to be delivered or digested in a single session, and the more obvious breaking points have therefore been indicated by asterisks.

Scriptural quotations are given in the *Jerusalem Bible* version.

A.N.

Contents

Preface

YEAR BY YEAR, the novices of the Little Brothers and Little Sisters of the Gospel go into the desert, to Beni-Abbès, where they spend the last weeks of their novitiate at the hermitage of their father and founder, Father de Foucauld. There, in the chapel built by Brother Charles of Jesus, they take their first vows. But before this, they make a retreat.

These talks were given to the Little Brothers and Little Sisters in March, 1971, to prepare them for this first step into the religious life. I publish them now in the hope that they may be useful to other young people preparing to enter religion. The talks were originally taped, and hence are not perhaps as polished as the reader might wish. Nor, unfortunately, can the written word convey the very special atmosphere in which the retreat took place, in the poverty and silence of that desert chapel where, more easily than anywhere else, we rediscover the spirit of the man whose example inspires our own vocation.

At a time when so many traditional and probably essential ideals of religious life are being called into question, I can only say that these same ideals, if we love them sincerely and simply instead of merely arguing about them, are still entirely valid. The gift of ourselves in the love of chastity, the imitation of the poverty of Christ, brotherly love, intimate union with the Son of God in prayer, true and living faith in his Eucharist, total devotion to the evangelisation of the poor: all this together forms an ideal never failing to bestow on those content to live it a boundless peace and joy in the certainty that they are living to their truest and fullest capacity. Young people, whatever their nationality, who take vows here and follow the way of Brother Charles, only differ from other young people of our day in one respect: that they have heard the call of Jesus and are doing their best to answer it. Beyond the changing fashions of the world, the Son of Man, crucified yet risen again, proclaims the same message heard by the first disciples in Galilee. The call of Jesus goes out to men of every century; it concerns man's inmost heart, summoning us to a destiny that no civilisation, no culture, has the power to alter.

I had just been writing this, when my attention was caught by something Peter Berger says in *A Rumour of Angels*: 'It seems reasonable to predict that secularisation will continue to spread. A mass-rediscovery of the supernatural is unlikely. Islands of supernaturalism will of course survive in secularised civilisation. Some of them will perpetuate a vestigial traditionalism ... Others, consisting of new groupings, will be the growing-points for a rediscovery of the supernatural. But these two types of island will have one feature in common: they will tend to adopt a more or less sectarian type of organisation. The major churches will persist in steering a middle course between traditionalism and *aggiornamento*: and so doing, will gradually be eroded by the sectarian tendency on the one hand, and the dissolving effects of secularism on the other. I am not being alarmist, but I think this is much more likely to happen than what our modern enthusiasts predict: be it the death of religion or, contrariwise, the resurrection of the gods.'

Berger's prediction may indeed be reasonable, but reasonable is precisely what the irruption of the Word of God in human history and the ways of his Kingdom are not. They keep confounding our calculations, just as they confounded the nationalism of the Jews, the philosophy of the Greeks and the might of Rome. The supernatural, whatever you may say about it, is intrinsically bound to the being of Christ, and to the life that he shares with us in his Body, the Church. The supernatural exists and will go on existing at the heart of the world and in the hearts of men. The problems arising in religious life could soon be solved, if we were absolutely clear in our own minds that such a way of life would be neither conceivable nor practicable, were it not for its basis in the supernatural. We cannot deny or question the existence of the supernatural and at the same time hope to maintain a secularised religious life: all we should have would be a building without foundations, a meaningless façade.

The only decisive answer to these problems lies in the joyous certainty of those who already know within themselves the fullness of life and truth found day by day in their 'Well-beloved Brother and Lord Jesus', to whom they have given all.

Beni-Abbès, March 25, 1972.
René Voillaume

I

Receiving the Call

THERE ARE MOMENTS, brief indeed, in everyone's experience that determine the whole future course of our life. They come when we once decide to commit ourselves to something for good. And that, Little Brothers and Little Sisters, is exactly what you have come to do here, in this chapel, where Brother Charles of Jesus lived a life of deep intimacy with Jesus. It was a very personal relationship, an extremely private one, if I may say so, the way Father de Foucauld lived here. Yet, it has had great influence on every one of us here, and indeed on the whole Church.

One by one, we come to the hermitage of Beni-Abbès to try our best to answer a call. At the same time, we cannot help being aware that the world and the people in it are very different today from when Brother Charles was living here. We belong to quite another world from the one that he knew. And since this is the case, we must necessarily wonder whether realities so intimately affecting the human heart as, for instance, giving our life to Christ, living in personal relationship with him, may also have been affected by these changes in the world. But the life led by St Teresa of Avila in the Carmelite convents of Spain, or by St Thérèse of the Child Jesus at Lisieux several hundred years later, or by St Francis of Assisi in thirteenth century Umbria, or by Brother Charles of Jesus here in the opening years of our own century—I mean their experience of union with God—is one and gloriously the same. And this is

what you too are now called to share. At this level of life with
Christ how could anything have changed?

But how, you will ask, as you wait in simple faith and
abandonment to the Lord to be cast like seed into the world,
like leaven into the dough, how can lowly human beings reach
such heights? What you treasure most inwardly, what nourishes
your own inner life, will probably seem to you alien to the
world, often denied by it and of no interest to most people who
often will not understand what you are doing. Naturally you
will wonder about your vocation: what it means and why.

* * *

First of all I want to talk about vocation as implying a call from
God. When we talk of a call like this, we must first consider
whether it is real or not. The idea of vocation pre-supposes
some notion of God's relationship with man, about Christ's
relationship with each of us as individuals. If there really is a
call, it is the beginning of something vital, something new
between him and us, which must have a great effect on our
own life. That God should address his call to us must make us
re-examine our relationship with Jesus, the very purpose of our
life, our share in the work of spreading the Gospel and the
duties to be ours among men.

You come from different countries, different environments,
different family backgrounds. You come from all over the place,
but here your paths cross. You have all led completely different
lives. You may even find it hard to understand one another,
since you do not all speak the same language. So, why are you
all here? We must try and find out why this should be, since, if
we have all come in answer to a call from God, this call must
have something in common for all of us. You will of course go
on being different from one another, but what God is giving
you, what he is going to give you, and what you must be willing
to accept from him, is what is to draw you together and, more
than that, make you one. Everything from God tends towards
unity. In this hermitage there is a cell dedicated by Brother
Charles of Jesus to the Apostle Peter; among other texts that
he put on the walls, he chose Christ's words: *There will be only
one flock, and one Shepherd.*

Obviously this gathering into one flock does not mean that

all men have got to become alike nor, as far as you yourselves are concerned, that you have all got to be cast in the same mould. There was a time in the religious life when undue importance was attached to outward uniformity, sometimes even seen as a mark of perfection. All the same, if Jesus calls you, to give you something in common, you have a duty to find out what it is, since the gift must be actively accepted: it belongs to each of you, it is personal to each of you, and at the same time it is shared, being common to all.

You have come here from various countries and you have come because God wished you all to meet in one single vocation. You are wondering what you are henceforth to make of your life, and in what way it is going to be different from the life of other Christians. You have been singled out by a new call. Now you have to answer it. This willingness to listen and to answer is the root of the matter, for the moment we stop thinking of the religious life, the dedicated life, as the response to a call, we lose any sense of its true meaning. The religious life will always be the answer to a call. But to answer, we first have to know how to listen. If you answer without listening to the question, your answer may well be beside the point. It is not a matter of giving anything anyhow—even if whole-heartedly—but of responding to a specific call from God. Generosity, even heroic devotion, would not be enough. What we have to ask ourselves is what the Lord expects of us.

This concept of vocation is found throughout the history of the People of God. The story of salvation as revealed to us in Holy Scripture repeatedly shows us God intervening in human affairs by addressing his call to men. The very birth of the People of God was the effect of the answer to one such call, or rather of many answers to many calls. God calls a people, God calls the Church, God calls all men. But the call always leaves us our freedom of choice: that is what makes it something personal. You could not do better while you are here than to look up those passages in the Old and New Testaments telling of God's calls. Meditate on them, beginning with God's call to Abraham, right through to the calls addressed by Jesus to the men and women around him. Abraham's vocation was founded on a call from God, so was that of Moses, and that of the prophets.

But, you will probably object, these were very exceptional people, giants whom God needed, his plan being to use men to lead men. Agreed: but I do not think as regards the actual calling that there is any essential difference between their vocations, marked by such huge breadth of mission, and our own. There is however a difference between the calls of the Old Covenant and ours, since under the New Covenant, since the Incarnation of the Word and the founding of the Church, the calls come from Jesus, and hence every vocation always leads us to work with him. Ours are calls delivered by Jesus Christ, in Jesus Christ and for Jesus Christ. That makes them different. John the Baptist himself still belonged to the Old Covenant, and he was called by the Lord to go into the desert to prepare the way for him from whom henceforth all calls would come. After John the Baptist, Jesus calls in person: he called his apostles, his disciples, he called and never stops calling a host of men and women for every sort of mission, with him during his lifetime and later in the Church. All vocations now come from Christ and therefore through his Church, and all have the same purpose, to build the Body of Christ.

You will find it easy to reflect on some of these vocations, better known to us because of their greater importance in the history of the Church. Take, for instance, Saul of Tarsus who became Paul and whose life was turned upside down by the One whom he was persecuting. Take Francis of Assisi, Catherine of Siena, Teresa of Avila, Joan of Arc, Dominic, Thérèse of the Child Jesus, Brother Charles of Jesus or any other saint or apostle, and you will find that their lives, their vocations exhibit the same characteristics. Men and women cannot commit their lives so uncompromisingly to God's service unless in response to a call, a call commanding too much respect for its contents to be modified later. When Christ calls us, he calls us to entrust us with a mission; we cannot go on living as we please. We must never forget: ever since the Word was made flesh and the Church was founded, every vocation has to come from Jesus Christ. We could say that thenceforth every vocation is a call to follow Jesus more nearly, to work with him more closely, making his aims our aims, his purposes our purposes. And so we are caught up for good in, can never again escape from, the high adventure of the Incarnation.

We shall often have to mention the polarities and tensions characterising Christian and religious life: action and contemplation, serving God and serving man, apostolic labour and prolonged prayer, solitude and human relations. Why these polarities, why these conflicts between apparently contradictory activities? Why this duality apparently conflicting with any unity of purpose in ourselves? This is something beyond our power to change, since it reflects two essential elements of the Gospel message, by which we approach a double mystery of communion—communion of the most intense degree. Man can only develop fully when in communion with others. Now, in Jesus, the Word has taken flesh to lead us all into the most intense communion with God—communion so intimate that no rational being would ever have conceived of such a thing, or desired it. Every human being is called to communion with his God—an everlasting communion, filial on the one hand, divine on the other. This is one aspect of the mystery.

The other is an equally intense communion of men with each other. This is the communion of brothers, but it, too, is divine and we are led to it by the Son of God made man. Jesus draws us to join him in deeper, closer communion with our brothers than we could ever have imagined for ourselves. Every Christian community, every religious community, is an ecclesial community gathered together round Christ; each forms a society drawing men closer to each other, forging new relationships, more intimate and more exacting than we can ever completely discharge.

Such then are the two intense communions to which the Gospel invites us. And this is why every vocation, every call coming from Christ is inevitably characterised by these polarities, one towards intimacy with our God, and the other towards intimacy with our brothers. Father de Foucauld called Jesus 'his well-beloved Brother and Lord', and called himself 'Little Brother of all', to show the relationships that were henceforth to link him to Jesus and to his brother-men.

I have chosen to talk of vocation in terms of this dual communion, so that we shall not be tempted, as people sometimes are, to think of vocation as a purely personal matter. People often talk of 'having a vocation' as though it were a private possession exclusively their own. But this is not so. You have received your vocation from Christ as an urgent invitation to commit yourselves more totally to him, which is to say, to communion with God and with your brother-men. Even the most absolutely contemplative vocations, by the very fact of their remoteness from worldly affairs, tend towards a more imtimate communion with men: only the means are different. Every vocation therefore implies a call to participate more completely in the mystery of Christ, in intimate communion with him, and hence, in him, with his Father and with Christ's brother-men.

You will now have a clearer idea of the sort of questions that you ought to be asking and which I must try to help you to answer, about the substance of the call coming to you from Jesus through Brother Charles of Jesus in our Fraternity. If these questions remain unresolved, you will not be able to respond perfectly to your vocation in the life now stretching before you. This life will hold different, unpredictable experiences for each of you, depending on which fraternity you join, on the people to whom the Church sends you, and on what you yourselves are now and what you will be, as the choices you make, and as circumstances, may determine. As followers of Christ, you will have to suffer, but with him you will also experience great joy. With Christ you will penetrate the very mystery of human destiny. Yet, however your individual vocation works out, the self same call of God will keep you united in a single spiritual family imbued with an identical spirit in all its undertakings. The call is not heard once for all; it will keep coming to you through the ordinary, humdrum, lowly circumstances of life. We shall never be done with deciphering the contents of the call; the Lord does not give it to us all at once like a programmed task, still less by revelation too plain to admit further doubt or discussion. We are labouring under an illusion if we think that God is likely to reveal his plan for us in some obvious way or by some action changing the course of history or one impinging on the normal course of daily life for us and everyone around us. No, God's voices are everywhere. But among the many voices talking the daily language of the world, there are God's voices addressed individually to us and not to anyone else. The deeper we plunge into our inner self, the purer—forgive the expression—will the voice of God and the voice of Christ sound on our inner ear—an intimate, friendly presence abolishing all anonymity in our relationship with the Unique Friend who has made us in his own image. To so personal a call, you have no choice but to answer throughout your life, calling you as he does through the Fraternity. The main subject of this retreat will be what this call holds for you; in this first talk I want to distinguish the general characteristics common to every vocation. And for these we must turn once more to the Bible, where we shall find both in the Old and the New Testament what the essential, unvarying characteristics are of calls from God.

In every case of vocation, God is always the one who takes the initiative. No one has ever gone in search of the Lord to say: 'Here I am, send me, use me.' Sometimes people have put themselves forward, but these exceptions prove the rule. The Lord is of course free to accept them, but as often as not he sends them about their business, like the scribe who offered to follow him in St Matthew, or the Gerasene demoniac in St Luke. God's call is always unsolicited, comes first. I cannot see how it could be otherwise, since the Lord himself disposes all things and all creatures, whether by his ordinary providence (often to our bewilderment) in world history as in our own lives, or by that providence effected by the direct operation of Christ on the hearts of his individual brothers and sisters. The certainty that we sometimes feel of having heard, deep within us, the call of God, is no illusion. A true call imposes order on the jumble of circumstance; it illuminates and fortifies the will. This call always comes first. It proceeds from Love and can only lead us to greater love. And in love we must respond.

Here again we find this two-fold communion, towards which all love must tend in the heart of a man redeemed and made god-like in Christ. Each overture made by God can only commit us more deeply to loving God and to loving men, because God is love, because Christ came to embody love, and the purpose of his life, his death and his resurrection was to unite us more deeply lovingly to his Father and to our brothers, and to make us freer than before—for, were we not free, his purpose would be frustrated.

Every call from God is a free gift bestowed on us by God. It is not for us to make comparisons between us. We must not do that. We each have the right before God to think of ourself as truly privileged. We do not know what gift God has given to our brothers, but we do know what he has given to us by calling us to the religious life; that is certainly a free gift, for which we are fully answerable: God entrusts himself to our freedom. Every gift given by God is given for love, and we shall have to show a return, not to mention the demands and duties that go with it. We must take the Parable of the Talents to heart. We must not underrate the demands made by a call from God: God asks for our whole life. We cannot answer him by halves. We shall soon see what the consequences are of dedicating ourselves to the Lord. God being love, he is demanding, terribly demanding.

Once again I refer you to Holy Scripture, repeatedly telling of the demands that God makes on his people and on those whom he has chosen to guide or to warn them. When God calls, he means to be obeyed; he demands everything, will share nothing. The prophets often described him as a jealous God. Yes, God is jealous—of each one of you. This is a true statement of our relationship with God, even though the anthropomorphic concept of a jealous God needs some thought before we grasp its deeper meaning. God's jealousy is one of the commonest themes in the Bible, and truly instructive on the demands of a God who will later reveal himself as Love.

From you, the Lord will expect no less than a love giving yourself entirely to him. What the Lord wants is you. Jealousy is only possible where there is love between people. God is jealous because he wants to be loved before all, and because he wants to love us. Indeed, he insists on our allowing him to love us. And here I am not speaking only of ourselves as individuals, nor of an individualistic approach to religion—for our whole apostolic mission is to serve this jealous love, the property of which is universal, embracing all mankind with equal jealousy. To serve this love, the Lord calls us to work with him in the apostolate of the Church. Though God's jealousy is unconfined, it fastens on the individual heart with all the fury of love that brooks no rival. The only reason that we deserve this love, is that God himself loves us. He comes first. Being loved by God is something very serious; advances like his demand a serious answer. We must never forget it.

This being so, every vocation results in the sealing of a covenant between God and the one who has been called. In other words, we are individually committed to observing that new and everlasting Covenant sealed in the blood of Jesus. Whenever God calls his servants, he invites us, each according to our circumstances, to implement the Covenant struck once for all in Jesus Christ between God and his people. The New Covenant is implemented in different ways, to differing degrees, in every vocation, and especially in every religious vocation.

All covenants depend on the fidelity of the contracting parties. The Lord, in making the first advances, pledges his fidelity. I think that nothing is more important for us than a truly unshakeable faith in the faithfulness of God, since this will give us the strength to answer him as faithfully. Changeable as we are, our own fidelity will take the form of promises as rich in value today as ever they were—psychological problems and intellectual objections currently evoked by fear of firm commitment notwithstanding. Our God is firm in his promises: God is constant, God is our Rock, God is the Faithful One. If you study the uneasy history of God's Covenant with his people, if you study the teachings of the prophets, you will find much to help you understand what is happening on the more personal level, between you and the Lord who calls you to make a Covenant of religious profession with him.

And here I must remind you that we are living in the days of the Church; she is the medium, by virtue of the mission she holds from Jesus, through which every covenant, every dedication, comes to its true fruition. Your call to be a Little Brother or Little Sister, coming as it does from Jesus, can only be fulfilled in the Church. Nothing coming from Jesus can reach us now except through the Church. Hence our vocation cannot be properly understood except by the light and fervency of our faith in the mystery of the Church.

You have certainly been thinking all these things over since the call from Jesus led you to the Fraternity more than a year ago. Now that you are here, you must think about them again as they affect you personally. For the time has come to give a clear answer to the succession of calls that you have been hearing all your life. You must call them all to mind today, so that you can discover what they mean. You must be sure that these calls are bidding you follow Brother Charles of Jesus by pledging yourself to one very specific way of life. God does not guide us in the abstract, or in some vague way. God is never in the abstract—that is impossible. Indeed, in a certain sense, God is infinitely concrete in his presence and in his actions. God reveals himself in the most personal circumstances of life. Each living being is unique; existence makes us so. And we are 'the living', now. Isn't it astonishing to think, that throughout human history there have never been two people exactly alike, and that there never will be? No life can ever be exactly like another. Every life develops differently. The Lord, working in the hearts and lives of his saints, in the hearts and lives of everyone of us here, is doing something by its nature completely concrete and personal. Freely to co-operate with him, as you ought, you must discover which way God is leading you, so that you will be able to respond whole-heartedly to the promptings of the Holy Spirit. You are pledging your life, not just part of your life but your whole life undivided. To make reservations would not be worthy of his summons. A religious, apostolic vocation does not consist in performing a set task, or in 'working to rule', or in devoting so many hours of the day to the Master and keeping the rest for ourselves, like a wage-earner going home after a day's work, feeling that he has done his duty by his employer. Not at all: we are proposing to give ourselves, our whole life, to God. We cannot keep anything back for ourselves, and responsibility for our lives henceforth rests in the hands of Christ, of the Church, and of the superior of the Fraternity before whom, our hands in his hands, we shall have pronounced our vows.

2

Foundations of Religious Life

LAST TIME, WE were talking about vocation as a call from God, dominating and marking our lives forever. We must now consider how we are to answer the call—for we are free to answer or refuse. We want all sorts of things, we make plans, we try to work out what exactly it is that we want; it was our own choice to join the Fraternity and by so doing we have chosen a particular kind of life. We shall still always be free, and Christ only wants to make us freer still: for to love we must be free. We have chosen an ideal by which we hope to live our lives, and we believe that the Lord has prompted us to this. Even so, we shall have to keep adapting our plans to meet God's plans of which we are not yet aware; we may even have to revise them, since the Lord speaks to us not only in the recesses of the heart but also, century after century, by revealing himself again and again in human history. He speaks to us in the Scriptures, he speaks to us through his Church, he speaks to us through his saints. The Spirit of God is at work, not only in us but in our brothers and in the Church. And this is particularly relevant to what we are going to think about now: a life vowed to the Lord and entirely dedicated to serving him in the Church.

Even in something as individual and personal as our vocation, there cannot be contradictory instructions and promptings proceeding from one and the same Spirit. The bewildering contradictions which we sometimes seem to encounter arise from the weakness of our understanding when confronted by the realities of God, and from the mistakes that we make in interpreting our feelings and what we suppose to be the promptings of the Spirit. And again, how can we rely exclusively on our own judgment, when we do not even know where we are going? I repeat, we do not know where we are going, nor where the Lord means to take us.

When the Lord called the apostles and they began to follow him, they did not know where they were going, even if they may have thought they knew. They let themselves be led by the Lord, and we in our turn must learn like them to let the Lord lead us. Christ's teachings and the content of our Christian hope notwithstanding, we are still in the dark about the ulti- mate meaning of human life, of the apostolate and of the Church. We have a natural tendency to argue and debate about such matters, and in the process we destroy as much as we claim to construct. On one occasion Jesus said to Peter:

> When you were young,
> You put on your own belt
> And walked where you liked;
>
> But when you grow old,
> You will stretch out your hands,
> Ane somebody else will put a belt round you
> And take you where you would rather not go.

By this, he meant Peter to understand that life would lead him to a fate that he had not foreseen and that he would find painful to accept. Is it possible to fulfil our vocation as followers of Jesus, without learning to 'go where we would rather not go'? Illusion and inexperience beset us when it comes to follow- ing Jesus, and we cannot do it unless we accept him as master of our plans and guide of our actions. And this requires that we be ready and willing to make any renunciation and any sacri- fice, even that of life itself. And this is particularly true of the demands made by life in religion.

*　*　*

You are about to pledge your life in its entirety. The Church will receive your pledge as an act of dedication to the religious state. You must therefore understand exactly what the religious life is. And this is all the more important since, even though you may not now be asking questions about it but in simplicity of heart accepting it as the Church offers it, you cannot help being aware that today the fundamental principles of religious life are under attack, and that the temptations and doubts assailing so many members of religious orders may one day also assail you. Nothing is worse than to start reappraising an ideal, once we have dedicated our life to it. Other considerations apart, we should always be trying to understand more about what we are doing and why.

We must think of the religious life—to quote the last Council —as a gift bestowed by God on his Church: notwithstanding the many imperfections inevitably due to the fact that it has to be lived by men. Clearly then, the religious life is a work of the Holy Spirit, and could not exist, were men and women not called by the same Spirit to give themselves willingly and completely to Christ. No one can impose the religious life on anyone else. No man can make another adopt it.

What is the religious life then, as others see it? Simply this: that Christians have decided to live together so that they can devote themselves to specifically spiritual activities or to those concerning the Kingdom of God. Some lead a life of solitude and prayer, others devote themselves to various types of apostolate, or to various ways of relieving human suffering, in the service of their fellow men. This is what the religious life looks like from outside. And although this view of it is incomplete, it is basically correct, since all religious life certainly involves a more or less exclusive dedication to activities more or less directly concerned with that mysterious entity known as the Kingdom of God. We shall have more to say about this later. The religious life is also led in community, vocations to the eremitical life excepted. It is also a life in which we are bound by promises and by obedience to a rule: that is why it is called stable and firm. Next, it is a life involving what is called the profession of the evangelical precepts: which under one form or another means practising the three precepts of chastity, poverty and obedience. And lastly, as a result of all this, it is a life that the Church recognises as dedicated.

With many variations, such has been religious life throughout the Church's history. Born as it were spontaneously of the breath of the Spirit, and its authenticity guaranteed by the

Church, the Church continues to hold it up to us, affirming its value amid the conflicting objections of the modern world. And today, as you know, religious life arouses many objections.

In opposition to this traditional view of religious life, there is a modern tendency to deny any specific difference between the secular Christian life and the dedicated one. As for the teaching and social work which used to be regarded as the province of Religious Institutes, people are more and more aware, and in most cases quite rightly, that you do not have to be in religion to undertake these. Then again, the dedicated religious life is called into question on the grounds that the only true dedication is that conferred by baptism. And stability, to the modern way of thinking, looks more like a fault than a virtue. Many people, aware of their own weakness, do not feel that they should commit themselves finally and firmly, at the same time taking the view that stability is contrary to the mobility and drive indispensable to any form of progress. Or again, religious rules no longer seem to encourage stable commitment, owing to the changes that they themselves are undergoing and the convulsions wracking many a congregation in search of its proper function in the contemporary world. How can you commit yourself to a community for good, when you cannot be sure that it will be the same tomorrow as it is today? People do not see what making a promise has to do with evangelical perfection. Submitting to the discipline of a rule seems repugnant to spontaneity, to creative originality, to individual responsibility, to a readiness to respond to the needs of our neighbour, or to events—all of which seems more important than making a promise. Living and getting on with the job, that is the main thing, not making promises. As for the three precepts, though these have long been sanctioned by the tradition of the Church, and have been regarded by the Church as constituting the religious state, some people now wonder whether this is indeed beyond debate. These precepts being addressed to all Christians—so the argument runs—should be lived by all, and there is no need to be in religion to do that. Or again, the secularising movement, sometimes even repudiating the dedicated life altogether, holds that the only true form of dedicated life is to be found among the laity, living in the world and doing their ordinary jobs. As for the Church's teaching on the religious life, and especially the last Council's very explicit declarations in the Constitution *Lumen Gentium* and the Decree *Perfectae Caritatis*, these two are food for debate, some people claiming that they should only be regarded as a basis for further theological research, and as merely marking one particular stage in the evolution of Christian thought. All the more so, they add, since the religious life is by nature spontaneous and charismatic, and since the Church, given that she has the right to pronounce on the fruits of religious life, has no right to lay down rules for it, and even less to decide in which direction it should develop. Among all the other difficulties confronting religious institutes in their efforts towards renewal, this doubt cast on the very essence of the religious state has caused the worst confusion. People are no longer willing to accept the teaching and guidance of the Church.

I cannot enlarge on this subject in the course of a retreat; all the same you should certainly be aware of the existence of those views on the nature of the Church and of religious life. The Holy Spirit's activity in the Church is held to be essentially dynamic, meaning that everything is always new and in a sense unpredictable. It is not the hierarchy's function—these theologians maintain—to say what form the renewal of religious life should take, but merely, once that renewal has taken place, to analyse and ratify what the Holy Spirit has already done. Without going quite as far as that, many Christians and many religious are letting themselves be influenced, more or less consciously, by these or similar ideas, supposedly more attuned to the modern mind, the social sciences and the political evolution of society.

This is a somewhat simplified picture; I hope it is not too gloomy. You are however aware of the unhappy state of affairs in many religious congregations, and of how reappraisals conducted without proper recourse to the light of faith produce no fullness of life or Christian joy. And speaking of joy, I must remind you how important joy is in a life specifically directed towards contemplation of God, the source of all happiness: in a way of life based on a literal interpretation of the Beatitudes, as Christ proclaimed them. We have to dare to direct our lives towards that happiness. The saints radiated an immense happiness around them. How easy it is, even in the religious life, to lose sight of the joy that comes from sacrifice, of the joy that comes from poverty (which shone so marvellously in the heart of the Poor Man of Assisi), and of that fullness of life of the man made new in Christ, crowning the lives of so many religious unafraid of mortification and renunciation.

And this is why I am asking you to reflect on certain values of the Christian life—perforce even more pertinent to the religious life, since that is Christian life lived to the full. We must not be frightened by these modern trends; in the long run, they, too, will have had their value by making us reaffirm the basic elements of our religious life with deeper, clearer understanding and therefore renewed conviction.

Hence the relevance now of re-affirming certain of the values of Christian life. A concept of Christian life that excluded religious life and could no longer engender it in its various basic types, would be spurious. It is the very nature of Christian life to give birth to religious life among the People of God. Were Christian life no longer capable of flowering into religious life, this would be a sure sign that some of the qualities most fundamental to it had been lost.

Let us therefore take three points as a basis for our further reflexions. The first is that Christian life has its roots in the death and resurrection of Christ; the second is the coming of the Kingdom of God and how this affects the world; and the third is the question, whether there is such a thing as evangelical perfection and what its essential characteristics are.

* * *

For us, the double event of the death and resurrection of Christ is central not only to the history of salvation but to all human history. Though not apparently influencing the ordinary course of events in the least, it has the profoundest implications for the destiny of man, conferring on him an other-worldly dimension, entailing a true transfiguration of spiritual life beginning here below. Instead of using such expressions as 'Christ's redemptive work', 'Christ the Redeemer', and 'the reconciliation of man to God', it is now more fashionable to talk about 'the liberation of man'. This can be perfectly appropriate, but is not without ambiguity, since it is often used to mean the organised efforts made by trade-unionists, politicians and indeed revolutionaries —not excluding recourse to violence—to liberate men from injustice and oppression by-the state or other institutions. There is therefore a risk of overlooking the distinction between this often justifiable, temporal activity, and the other sort of liberation springing from the death and resurrection of Jesus. Clearly, when Jesus says: 'I am the Resurrection and the Life', he is taking us far beyond earthly things, and far beyond a world 'that is passing away'. He is talking about life eternal.

If you observe the meaning of sanctification, you will see a great truth here. If Jesus is the Word made flesh, if Christ, by passing through death, conquered death and was glorified, the reason was that the glory which he had with God, as Word from all eternity, transfigured his humanity. This is a great mystery, with incalculable effects on the future life of every human being. The mystery is wonderfully signified and transmitted to every Christian by baptismal regeneration. Thence follows a true transfiguration of human nature, though this is temporarily indiscernable, the implanted grain of glory working invisibly, yet continually deep in the heart. The time of glory will not come while we are here on earth. All is hidden, secretly waiting. Human life and human history go on just the same: just as they did before us, just as they will after us. The glory of eternal life buried in the heart of the Church is no more visible to our eyes than the glory of the Word was visible in the humanity of Christ while he was living on earth. The Son of Man had to pass through death before he entered into glory. This is what we are always forgetting. The transfiguration, the divinisation in store for us, requires that we do not forget—as well we might amid the distractions of the world—the presence of a reality which we call supernatural, since it is divine and eternal. Admittedly, the word 'supernatural' is scarcely respectable today. Is this because every generation needs a new vocabulary, needs to discard worn-out words and give language new life and strength? Very probably: but we should remember that certain words express certain ideas; if we change the words, we may change the ideas too and so forget the truths that the words originally conveyed.

The supernatural destiny that Christ bids us enter with him means supreme, unimaginable self-fulfilment. I use the word in its truest sense: I mean, fulfilment of our nature and our life in every way that we could desire and indeed beyond everything that we could conceive. Whether it be on the plane of love, or of truth, or of nature, or of life, we can truly say with the Apostle Paul: 'We proclaim the things that no eye has seen, and no ear has heard, things beyond the mind of man, all that God has prepared for those who love him.' No words ever can express 'things which must not and cannot be put into human language'. Without this vision of man's transfiguration by Christ and in Christ, Christianity has no meaning.

But transfiguration does not take place without our playing our part. God has created us with freedom of choice. The transfiguration promised to us in Christ requires our co-operation. And the transformation produced in the Christian heart, as a result, while we are still on earth, is none other than the holiness that sets us free from evil and sin so that we may become one with Christ.

Here I might say in passing that, just as people today regard knowledge of the past as irrelevant to our more and more scientifically-orientated civilisation, so this same attitude of mind can easily be adopted by Christians towards the tradition of the Church, at the very moment when tradition has so much to offer towards the renewal of Christian and religious life.

The Holy Spirit has been at work in the human heart ever since man first appeared on earth, as also through countless generations of saints and Christians. The Holy Spirit does not necessarily keep saying what he has said already: since what he has already said, he has already entrusted to the Church. That same Spirit, for whom we are listening today, is the author of that same wisdom, of which the Church is the constituted guardian, which she has a mission to hand on to us, and which we have a duty to receive. Imagine our plight, our spiritual poverty as regards our knowledge of God, if we, ignoring the accumulated wisdom of the centuries, were to begin all over again with each successive generation. But this is unfortunately what we are often tempted to do, not exactly deliberately, but under the influence of current fashions of thought. The resulting impoverishment can prevent us from responding to this ideal of fullness in Christ, fullness of eternity and ultimate source of joy and happiness for men.

So, coming back to the concept of the supernatural, this is what the word means, in the sense that man is called to be more than he is. Such, henceforth, in Jesus is the destiny of man. So do not let us be afraid of the word 'supernatural', nor of the truth that it expresses, obliging man to believe that he must reach out towards a perfection beyond his stature.

The mystery of the death and resurrection of Jesus has no meaning except in terms of eternal life for man, and hence of a real transfiguration of our earthly condition. Seen in this light, the Kingdom of God—about which we are going to talk next— begins to take a clearer shape. We are at the very heart of the problem now preoccupying Christendom.

* * *

Thanks to scientific progress, we are able to study the history of the world and our history on it, although, as concerns the latter, our investigations may produce only conjectural answers. We try to foresee and plan our future scientifically. But thanks to these very scientific methods, we are trapped inside our own history and inside cosmic history, not knowing how to escape the limitations of either. Who will give us the knowledge of the things of God, given that they exist? And what indeed are the things of God? Is the world, revealed by scientific analysis and experienced by us as a tangible reality, the unique reality, or is it not? The Christian affirmation that there is another reality beyond the scope of scientific investigation has little in common with general attitudes today.

Without trying to predict the future of mankind, we can easily foresee the day when man will have become so conditioned by ideologies encouraging him to assume ever-increasing control over his own development, and so mentally strait-jacketed by scientific disciplines claiming to account for every aspect of his nature, that he will find it very hard, perhaps even impossible, to speak of the things of God, or to know or understand what they are. When we think of all the supernatural truths both present and to come that Christ conveyed in those simple words 'Kingdom of God', we have to confess that he meant very much more than one particular recipe for procuring a just, and therefore peaceful, society on earth, even though the coming of the Kingdom of God in its fullness entails and demands our efforts in this direction. The Kingdom, as Christ inaugurates it and sees it, is something much vaster, extending beyond things visible.

A few moments ago, I mentioned the Church and its past. Now, the Church's past is not, as you might think by analogy with human history, a mere memory of events long vanished but for the written word, nor of truths set down in the documents of distant Councils, nor of a spiritual heritage preserved in the history of religious orders. A dead past, would you say? Or is it an invisible part of the Kingdom of God, and very much alive? The apostles, martyrs, holy popes and holy bishops, all the saints known or unknown to us, who have woven the history of the Church, make up a world of living beings. Whether or not there are hosts of angelic creatures, blessed spirits and saints, living in the glory of Christ, is not irrelevant to a proper conception either of the Kingdom of God, or of Christian life today. Too many Christians and too many religious think that this is not particularly relevant to human life on earth. But they are wrong. It is extremely relevant as far as the religious, and above all the contemplative, life is concerned. More than any Christian life, the dedicated life must reflect the fullness of the Kingdom of God, including that part of the Church already perfected in glory. The religious state prefigures the glorious state to which the human race is led by the grace of Christ; hence it should reflect what has already been fulfilled in the world of the angels and the blessed in expectation of the Resurrection. This, the major part of the Kingdom of God, truly exists; every life dedicated to Christ is orientated towards it. The last Vatican Council made this point several times, emphasising, as the Church had never done before, that the religious life is a sign of the realities present and to come of the Kingdom of God—such a way of life having no meaning, were these realities not real.

You see now why the religious has to bear witness among men to the reality of the Kingdom of God; for men, being busy with the things of this world, need to have the invisible realities of the Kingdom made visible and tangible for them by their being embodied in other human lives.

*   *   *

What the Church has always taught and goes on proclaiming to the modern world about eternal life, human immortality, the glory of the saints, the existence and splendour of the angels, is completely at odds with contemporary thought. A tissue of myths no longer worth taking seriously? And we may as well admit that the crude, imaginative and anthropomorphic forms with which earlier generations clothed these highly spiritual and therefore unimaginable realities must bear some of the blame for this. Beyond the visible world and living beings that we can touch, know and understand, the light of God inducts us by faith into an infinitely vaster world of spiritual beings infinitely grander, more intelligent and nearer to the Lord than we are. In this wider vision of Creation and Redemption, our hope of a glorious and eternal life can come to fullest flowering.

And we now also see the nature of evil, of sin, in a new light. Are the rebel angels, Evil, Satan, also figures in a myth? The mysterious and dolorous work of redemption, embodied in the life of Jesus, we interpret as a victory over the Powers of Darkness. And again, given the reality of a world of spiritual beings, the existence of Satan's angels seems no more inconceivable than the mysterious way in which evil exerts such a hold over mankind in defiance of all reasonable explanation. The existence of angelic and demonic creatures puts the problem of evil into clearer perspective within the grand design of creation and redemption.

The problem of evil is always with us and the 'reign of sin' is far from over. Yet the word 'liberation' has never been more constantly used than today. We may, I fear, be in danger of forgetting what it really means. The final petition of the Lord's Prayer, in which we ask to be 'delivered from evil', has been interpreted in many ways. The 'evil' from which we pray our Father to deliver us, can be understood to mean the Spirit of Evil, the Evil One, Evil personified.

What is truly discouraging for the human intellect with its urgent need to know things, is that the invisible world never becomes visible, remaining shrouded in silence, ever beyond our reach. God himself never speaks, the dead never speak, the angels never speak, the existence of the Spirit of Evil can be disputed, can be denied with impunity: nothing compels us to attribute the ravages of wickedness and the proliferation of sin to the influence of diabolic spirits. This is true: and certain disquieting cases excepted, it will always be hard—and profitless—to decide how much the Spirit of Evil influences our actions, and how much we ourselves are to blame. We cannot cross the frontier separating the two worlds, earthly from invisible, temporal from eternal. You remember the parable about Lazarus, the poor man who was transported to Abraham's bosom. Jesus tells us that the frontier cannot be crossed: 'Between you and us,' said Abraham, 'a great gulf has been fixed, to stop anyone, if he wanted to, crossing from our side to yours, and to stop any crossing from your side to ours.' Only faith in God's messengers—not those coming from the other world, but those raised up among mankind—can teach us something of the reality of that world beyond our own. 'If they will not listen either to Moses or to the prophets, they will not be convinced even if someone should rise from the dead.' The only person born here who came from that other world, is Jesus, the Word made flesh. That great impassible gulf is the mystery of death. To pass from one side of it to the other, we have to die; not even the Son of Man was exempt from this universal law. Death, seen from our shore, is a dead-end; seen from the other, it is a birth, an entry into a new life. Death has two faces, but a great gulf separates them from each other. Jesus himself knew the pangs of death, experienced the death-agony, he knew what it felt like to die, never seeing so long as he had one breath left that opposite shore which would have marked his entry into glory.

If we do not believe these things in complete sincerity of heart and with all the strength of faith, we cannot live as Christians, let alone practise the religious life—for this should be the very concentrate of Christian living. Faith in these fundamental Christian realities is basic to all religious life. And this same faith makes it possible for us to choose the religious life, in full awareness of what it involves. And you will only be able to live up to its demands, if you really understand what it means, as far as your own life is concerned, as far as the Church is concerned and as far as other men are concerned. A religious must see the Kingdom of God as a present reality, as something so concrete that we can really live for it. Our faith must be such that we can really and truly listen for Christ. He sees those things that are divine and invisible, we believe in them because He tells us of them. He is the Lord by whom all things were made. And we must put our eyes into Christ's eyes, our mind into his mind, our hands into his hands and let him guide us, even when we cannot see for ourselves or understand by light of our own intellect. That is what is meant by living by faith: referring everything to Christ—not to Christ as interpreted by such and such a commentator, forthwith contradicted by another, discussed by so-and-so and dismissed by someone else—but Christ as he has revealed himself century after century through the Church, Christ as he rises beyond all intellectual discussions, Christ as he has been loved, known and followed by generations of saints.

The Kingdom of God on the one hand: the reality of the world on the other. We cannot escape from the latter, immersed as we are in the tangible universe. The world then, is first, the sum of those realities subject to human knowledge, everything that can be perceived by our sciences and disciplines based on experience and verifiable by systematic experiment. In a word, the created, or more exactly the material, universe. When I say that we are imprisoned inside this universe, I am not saying that human intellect lacks all capacity for grasping, by intuition, the Truth that lies beyond visible reality. Far from it: that is the intellect's supreme function. But this particular dimension of the intellect can be so misunderstood or so neglected as to become virtually paralysed. Today's almost exclusive concentration on the rational sciences so deadens the capacity for grasping non-material truth, that we are reaching the point of hardly believing that the intellect is even capable of attaining to it. Any attempt to know things beyond the physical—that is to say, things metaphysical—is looked on as belonging to the order of poetic intuition. (And by poetry, people of course mean something purely imaginative and subjective.)

Then again, 'the world' has another set of connotations, comprising that enigmatic entity, the human race: how it works, what its past has been, what it is becoming and what its prospects are. Let us have another look at the Gospel, particularly at the Gospel of St John, and think about those passages dealing with 'the world'. St John was one of the disciples who knew Christ personally and, among all men of every age, the one who was closest to the heart and mind of Jesus. We ought therefore to attach the greatest importance to what he has to say. John bears witness to the Lord's thought in a way that no other man ever could. We should not rashly assume that the truths revealed by this trusted companion of Christ, were basically different then from the way they appear to us today. Admittedly, our scientific methods of investigation had not been discovered then; nonetheless, they were already latent, a potential dimension of human awareness. What is more, rationalistic and materialistic interpretations of the universe had already left their mark on human thought. The great questions about the meaning of life, suffering, death, social injustice, how society should be organised, politics, had already been asked. These various approaches, whether theoretical or practical, had already produced a variety of cultures and civilisations. So all that, too, is implied in the word 'world'.

We are in fact dealing with something very complex and hard to sort out, except by the light of faith. People today take what they call 'the values of the world' very seriously, and rightly so. The Church too, in *Gaudium et Spes*, has made a point of recognising the worth of this particular aspect of human life. But we are constantly in danger of forgetting how the same conciliar text qualifies this view of the world, by drawing attention to the ambiguity inherent in these values, however excellent they may appear to be. In the final analysis, the world is what man himself has made it, inevitably according to his own stature, and therefore as relative as he himself. The world, you might say, is what man has made out of the creation, and thus can never be greater than he is. The world will always be the reflection of what man is: an incomplete, divided being, on the one hand forever a prey to sin, evil and egoism, on the other capable of love, heroism and goodness and ever yearning for them. The world can give man nothing that he does not already possess, potentially at least. People today forget that the world is only relative: thinking and acting as though the world as it evolves will eventually be able to confer on them something more than they now are. Their view of how the world works encourages them to hope that man will be able to forge a destiny superior to what he is. Despite the inherent inconsistencies of this vision of the future, it does seem to be the only mystique capable of inspiring mass-movements in the modern world.

And now see how Christ himself speaks of 'the world': he uses the same word to mean something very different. And I do not think we shall make the matter any clearer by using different terms ourselves, since the matters in question are so intermingled as often to be different aspects of the same thing. In the end, it all comes back to the human heart. And that is the world that Christ redeemed and for which he died. 'God loved the world so much that he gave it to his only Son.'

And there is also a world, for which Christ refused to pray; from which he insistently begged his Father that his disciples should be preserved. Though he leaves them in the world, he does not wish them to be of the world. These are grave matters indeed, to meditate on by the light of Christ, for fear we never grasp the meaning of those renunciations that religious life exacts.

* * *

Now we come to our third matter for thought: the notion of evangelical perfection. Let us go back to the two-fold mystery of the death and resurrection of Jesus and the transfiguration of man that follows from it. The transfiguration is already complete; at the same time it is still to be completed. By virtue of Christ's resurrection, he imparts divine life and strength to his Church, and through her, by baptism, to every member of the People of God. But each of us for our part has to accept this transfiguring grace, and let ourselves be transformed by it: which cannot come about without our constant, courageous and willing co-operation. God cannot redeem us without our help. God cannot transfigure us unless we co-operate to the full. Each of us therefore has a task of self-perfection to perform; and the Gospel tells us what is to be done. Hence the term 'evangelical perfection'. We must not let the word perfection alarm us. In its primary sense it means that something ought to become better than it is at present: a thing is first improved, then perfected. Man is susceptible of improvement: he can and should perfect himself. The question then is to know just what this improvement should be, and how we should behave to perfect ourselves not only individually but collectively. Some people would be glad to hear the last of perfection; they find the very notion of perfection repugnant, having had it too often presented to them as a pre-conceived, pre-packaged ideal, or as the slavish imitation of some stereotype. The word and the ideal for which it stands have indeed often been debased. All the same, I do not see how we can do without the concept of perfection. Jesus himself said: 'You must be perfect just as your heavenly Father is perfect.' We must become perfect, that is to say, we must become perfectly in fact what we already are by right: men and sons of God. Men we shall certainly stay, even when we are bad ones, but we have a ceaseless duty to become what we are, since there is a law inscribed in the human heart that we can never stop trying to become more and better 'man'. This does not happen on its own. Nor is it achieved by merely changing people's living conditions or the existing social system. And this is the great mystery of the Church, that is to say, of Christ at work in the heart of every Christian.

The Lord has called you, with all other Christians, to evangelical perfection. This perfection cannot be achieved unless we observe certain conditions laid down by Christ himself—by his death and resurrection, which should be at work within us. Despite abuses arising in the past and despite jansenistic or puritanical distortions due to a misunderstanding of the part that love should play in a holy life: mortification, self-renunciation and the Cross are vital to the perfection of every Christian life.

The matters we are discussing are very serious ones; we must all realise that. Try as we may, we cannot eliminate the terrible reality of death. Death affects everything human. Even Christ had to pass through death before entering the fullness of his everlasting life of glory.

We cannot live a Christ-like life, unless we daily learn to die. There is nothing pessimistic about facing up to the reality of death; indeed it is extremely wholesome to do so. What is more, when man turns his back on this, when he tries to elude the mystery of death, he is soon lost. By rejecting death, he unwittingly rejects the law of his own life, the law of a fulfilled life. By only wanting to do what is pleasant and what is easy, by rejecting whatever entails and requires self-sacrifice, he arrives, not at self-perfection, but at self-destruction. Having free will, man has the fearful power of destroying himself. Yes, man can partially destroy himself, can diminish himself—just as he can perfect himself, or at least tend towards perfection, the perfection of those who live by the Gospel. I say 'tend' because the word implies 'tension': being pulled towards something, attracted, as though by inner compulsion, towards building the ideal man, embodied for every Christian in Christ. To reach that goal, we must be ready to do anything. This is the very work of salvation. The Apostle Paul uses the metaphor of the Olympic Games, of athletes tense to excel at their sports, undertaking the most rigorous training to win the prize. Everyone understood the application in St Paul's day, and it still holds good today.

When we come to talk more specifically about what constitutes the religious life, we shall have to show the relationship between this and the practice of the evangelical precepts. But first, what exactly are these evangelical precepts? And, more important still, are there any precepts in the Gospel?—for this is what people sometimes ask. Sometimes Jesus expressed himself in terms so forceful and so absolute that his teaching seems impracticable and even inhuman. 'If anyone hits you on the right cheek, offer him the other as well; if a man takes you to law and would have your tunic, let him have your cloak as well. And if anyone orders you to go one mile, go two miles with him.'

It has been pointed out that Christ did not himself obey these teachings to the letter. When for instance he appeared before Caiaphas, not only did he not turn the other cheek to the guard who struck him, but he reproached him: 'Why do you strike me?' And we could give other examples too. Why then take seriously and literally what is after all only a Semitic figure of rhetoric? Yet the disciples who first heard these teachings took them seriously, and after them generations of Christians, monks and religious from the days of the Desert Fathers to our own. Take away these teachings with their mysterious demands, and what is left of the divine novelty of the Gospel? We know all too well. The evangelical precepts as they are usually called, perfectly sum up the unlimited demands of the new law of love which Jesus came to reveal to us. Once the Christian has set out on the path of love, he will never be through with it. Driven by love, he must forever be ready to discover the new, concrete demands that it makes on his life, and to respond to these with ever-renewed whole-heartedness. This is what the precepts mean: that the law of love cannot be stated in limited commands, but always demands more of the man who, by accepting it, assents to being obliged to give without limit. These precepts of Jesus are like a code of love, the demands of which, being of their nature illimitable, keep urging us on to fulfil them in the most concrete ways, in practical terms, when we should often be only too happy to pause by the roadside and rest, with the thought that we had for the time-being done enough. The whole novelty of the Gospel is, as it were, summed up in this set of precepts addressed to all Christians. That is why the Council, when speaking of the precepts, does so in general terms and in the plural: since there is no end to them. From these teachings of Jesus forming an inseparable whole, tradition has however singled out three as essential, and as suitable foundations for a state of life to be called evangelical. We should not therefore regard as arbitrary a choice sanctioned by the constant tradition of the Church. These precepts are a true distillation of the Gospel, as indeed they are also of Christian experience.

Furthermore, you have only to consider what falls within the scope of the three precepts: chastity, poverty and obedience, to see that they embrace our entire life. When a Christian means to give himself to Christ by fulfilling the demands of these precepts to the uttermost, his whole life is involved: poverty affects his relationship with the rest of the world and his actions on created things; chastity lifts him above his deep-felt need for human love and fruitful home: and lastly, obedience takes away his independence and his right to decide what he will do in life and whom he will do it with. This means, in fact, a total takeover of a man's life by the Kingdom of God, he having bravely given it. The disciple of Jesus, thus set free, must be ready for each new demand made by the Spirit of God, and made by God's law, the law of love. The value of these precepts and their concrete effects on a man's life, were intuitively recognised by the early Christians, who first put them into practice. The tradition goes back to primitive Christian times and is therefore truly evangelical. We cannot make any substantial alteration without shattering the whole, as achieved when the precepts are put into practice. Suppress one of the three precepts and the sacrifice of a life to the Kingdom of God would no longer be a complete one. It is this very absoluteness of the gift that characterises the religious life.

The religious life is a Christian life affected by the Kingdom of God as to its outward living conditions—which in turn give rise to an environment—as also to all its undertakings altogether. The religious life is a reflection of the Kingdom of God, not only in its eschatological sense of something yet to come, but also in the other sense of something already invisibly present among men. If the religious life is not a gift in totality, it has no meaning, since only that which is absolute can convey the things of God. Hence the grandeur of the religious life and its importance in the Church. And this is why it cannot be lived, nor its demands even be understood, except by an act of living faith in the reality of the Kingdom of God. And here I am not talking only of that power of love placed by Christ in the heart of redeemed mankind to work on it like leaven in the dough, and to bring the Kingdom of God into being, in the sense that the Kingdom of God is among us. No, I also mean that other, invisible aspect of the Kingdom, where the souls of our dead and all the angelic creatures are united in hope and already in glory. The Kingdom of God is one and indivisible.

This vision of the Kingdom lies at the heart of Christianity. Without it, Christianity would offer a poor answer to human aspirations. If we, in an attempt to make Christianity palatable to modern taste, attenuate this vision of the Kingdom, we dilute the force of the gospel message, and then the gospel message stops being the light of the world, or the world's great hope, or the strength that men need to let themselves be transformed by the love of Christ.

Such briefly outlined are the three aspects of Christian life which I thought we ought to consider, for a clearer understanding of what we are going to say about the religious life. For it is impossible to commit yourself to this road unless you have deep conviction, a conviction that has to be all the stronger today since the relevance of this state of life is under fire, with impressive-looking appeals to reason being advanced against it. Though you yourself are inwardly convinced by the light of faith, you will still find yourself having to defend the ideal of evangelical life that you have embraced. You will have to be very strong and very clear-headed to stay loyal to these values, when others attack and deny them. Otherwise, it is better not to enter the religious life. For this cannot survive compromises; it is all or nothing. A watered-down religious life, a watered-down view of it on our part, would lose its Christian integrity, just as deliberate acceptance of infidelity and divorce destroys the Christian ideal of marriage. In either case, the demands are absolute and an essential consequence of the revelation of Love contained in Christianity. Of course, when we face such demands, Christ knows better than anyone how weak we are; we are sinners and always shall be. We shall always be sinful religious, just as married Christians will always be weak and sinful. But that is another matter. People often wonder how the religious life can be a perfect way of living in obedience to the Gospel, when we are all not only imperfect but sinful too. This is true even of the Church, but she is none the less the true Body of Christ even though all her members, including her ministers, are sinners. Isn't this one of the most bewildering and wonderful consequences of the Incarnation of the Word: to have set face to face, after disclosing them, the abyss of God's holiness, and the abyssal wretchedness of the human heart? One same Christ affirms the absolute claims of man's vocation to the heights of holiness, yet refuses to condemn the woman caught in the act of adultery. These two abysses meet in the heart of Christ the Saviour. Within the Church is a divine and holy presence far surpassing what its constituent members are capable of representing in their own lives. And the religious life too contains a reality surpassing the sum of the virtues practised by its constituent members. A Christian community is more than the sum of the men who are its parts, for 'where two or three meet in my name, I shall be there with them'.

3
Living in Brotherhood

IN THE GOSPEL, as we have said, Jesus shows us two very intense
and personal types of communion, between them comprising
the entire Christian vocation: a call to intimate, filial communion with God, and a call to achieve a brotherly intimacy
with our fellow-men in a relationship making virtually infinite
demands. This latter communion has to grow broader and
deeper as our communion with God grows more intimate.

We have been made in the image of God. Hence everything
Christian, everything supernatural, every gift given by God
to man, all these things—by the new light shed by Christ's
resurrection—we now find are the flowering and fulfilment of
an unsuspected longing deep in our own hearts. These deep-set
longings can be detected in the erratic and sometimes tragic
means adopted by men in their quest for self-fulfilment. Some
try to satisfy this need for communion with their fellows by
creating socialist communities. In the context of the modern
centralised state, they risk lapsing into collectivism or some
other form of society curtailing the basic freedoms of the human
spirit. Others, in contrast, try to escape the ruthless conditioning of society by taking refuge in a life of private intro-
spection, seeking a solitude in which they hope to find—as in
some inner paradise—that intimacy so tormenting in its
evasiveness, with Another. I doubt if this dual phenomenon
has ever been so widespread at any other period of history, or if
people have ever been more aware of it. And this being so, we

must now consider the essential element of religious life: living in community.

Christianity has a natural tendency to take the form of a community. We observe that the men and women who first received Christ's call to follow him spontaneously formed themselves into a community, without always realising, given their previous habits, just how deeply their new relationship bound them to one another. We witness the spontaneous creation of Christianity in that first Christian community in Jerusalem, described by St Luke in the Acts of the Apostles. This first expression of Christianity as a community, though short-lived, was important and has always been considered so by the Church. In the naïve and absolute form that the first disciples adopted and in their ignorance of the way in which human societies usually develop, they may have shown a certain lack of realism. None the less, that primitive community did embody in primitive freshness those values which should always be the distinguishing marks of any Christian community and, even more so, of every religious community.

Let us have another look at what St. Luke tells us about the way this first Christian society behaved, and about the spirit that pervaded it. Here we find a true reflexion of the Kingdom of God. Impregnated with the memory and teachings of the Master, the disciples had pooled their spiritual wealth: their faith in Christ their Lord, their joyful hope in his resurrection, their waiting for his return at the Second Coming. This preoccupied them so completely that nothing else mattered to them. Thenceforth, they held everything in common, they sold their possessions, and lived together in brotherly affection. This description does not seem to have been over-idealised, since the grave shortcomings that marked the enterprise from its very inception are also on record. But be that as it may, here we have the entire Christian community in essence: later to be the Church of the saints. The history of monastic spirituality shows us what nostalgia the finest religious have always felt for this first community in Jerusalem, regarding it as the perfect model of every religious community. It is the beginning of the Church, it takes pride of place, and it too will be perfected when the Church is perfected in the Heavenly Jerusalem. This is the ideal community towards which the human community tends, even though unawares. And we must consider what sort of religious community our Fraternity should be, taking this evangelical achievement as our example.

* * *

Here our first consideration should be that every individual has an absolute right to an environment allowing him to be truly himself and also to perfect himself. Man, like every other living creature, has to have an environment; this is a fundamental biological law. Everyone therefore needs a proper environment in which to live, to grow and to explore and develop his personality. It is a vital, absolute need. Very often, a man needs several environments: the environment of home, the environment where he works, the environment appropriate to his intellectual and technical training; and there is also an environment indispensable to all forms of mental activity, whether the theoretical sciences, the arts or even the religious life itself. If, people today have lost their bearings, the commonest reason is that the various environments in which they have to live are no longer adequate to ensure their complete and harmonious development. And more serious still, most of the environments in which people live today are unfavourable to any development of intellectual life. And brain-workers, possibly more than others, need the right kind of environment, as witness the unrest in our universities and in education more or less everywhere in the world.

We religious are not exempt from this general rule, being in fact called to a spiritual vitality more intense than any other. Religious life cannot exist and flourish without creating its own appropriate environment. And today, spiritual life is certainly suffering from a lack of environment. Again, the activities to which most religious are dedicated compel us to develop in all sorts of professional environments. Sometimes, a religious may find himself belonging to several environments at the same time: the one where he works, the one where he pursues his apostolate, while by virtue of being a dedicated man, he still needs his religious environment too. The degeneration affecting many religious environments, amounting in some cases virtually to extinction, is an irreparable disaster. One secularist school of thought even denies that the dedicated life needs a special environment. Yet, since no type of life or activity can develop or even survive without a minimally favourable environment, no more could a religious community reduce itself to the point of being indistinguishable from the Christian community of the laity—and still survive: even though the secularising movement sees no basic distinction between the two types of community. Indeed, you might as well abolish religious life altogether, since this cannot exist without its proper environment, that is, a community.

So, what is a religious environment?

One characteristic of any environment is that a number of people are gathered together in the name of a common ideal. But this is not enough. An environment should create living conditions appropriate to itself; an environment contains a spirit that it ought to be able to pass on to its members. An environment should also provide disciplines of life or work appropriate to its aims. Every environment is in fact a complex, human organism owing its existence to the fact that man is not designed to live alone. Common sense can be very illuminating here and often carries us further than we might expect. The importance of environment can be observed at every stage of the ladder of existence. Think, for instance, how careful you have to be if you want to grow a plant that can only thrive, flower and bear fruit in certain fixed conditions: you have to get everything right: soil, humidity, temperature, season, shade, sunlight. No two plants need quite the same environment. The same is true of different species of animal. Climatic changes, even very slight ones, make some species migrate; others even die out. And man too is an animal; one aspect of him is; and as, in addition, he has a spiritual life, a heart and an intellect, he needs a complex environment, an environment which only the company of his fellow-men can offer him. Every human environment is, when all is said and done, a community of brothers.

A religious environment should foster the development of the spiritual man who models himself on the Gospel. This is its essential characteristic. It ought to help the men and women who compose it to live in the spirit of the Beatitudes. It creates special living conditions, due to the practice of the three evangelical precepts. The outward characteristic of the religious community is a Christ-like poverty, and the attitude of sharing which comes from it. Another characteristic is that atmosphere of love and spirituality only generated by brothers united in dedicated chastity and obedience. You cannot do without this environment, if you mean to lead your religious life to the full. Man cannot be on his own; he cannot develop, grow and fulfil himself outside the network of relationships provided by the society of his brothers. No serious psychological study would deny this: quite the reverse. We know all about the inner conflicts and other psychological problems caused by inadequate environment, whether it be that of the family, or of those supposed to train and equip us for life. What countless people have been hopelessly maimed by their environment.

The religious environment must in a quite special way reflect the Kingdom of God, as instituted by Jesus Christ in its present earthly form; and also in its other-worldly form to come, for the accomplishment of which we must wait and work. I have introduced the subject of Fraternity life by talking about environment, because I consider this particularly important, living as we do at a time when human environments are no longer spontaneously created. In the old days, no one even gave a thought to such things, since the basic human environments seemed part of the natural order: family, clan, village, craft-guild, all offered the right conditions for normal human development. Similarly, parishes and religious communities formed environments adapted to their own purposes. Today, everything has to be re-thought, re-invented; progress itself drives us on, in spite of ourselves, to destroy those very living conditions needful to a truly human environment. Now that we have heard the psychologists' warning, we are having to set to work and rebuild the environments we need—this time artificially—or risk catastrophe. As we destroy the natural environment, forests, rivers, atmosphere, seas by polluting them all, so the spontaneously created human environments have been polluted too. The religious life has not escaped pollution either. The religious environment has degenerated, not merely because of its rigidity and its inability to adapt to new conditions, but more seriously because its very basis is now subjected to psychological objections on the one hand, and on the other

to new theological ideas calling the very nature of dedicated life
into question. How tragic for a religious not to be able to love
his community any more, and to feel that the house he shares
with his brothers, can no longer offer a brotherly atmosphere
capable of sustaining, strengthening and expanding his dedicated life! A cruelly traumatic situation for any man or woman
in religion, leading inevitably to the ruin of many a dedicated
life! So we must now think what the conditions of a religious
environment ought to be, and what the essential qualities are
of a community of brothers or of sisters gathered round the
Lord, to live in the spirit of the Gospel for the sake of the Kingdom of God.

Here we have to make the point straightaway that if the
environment in question is a community, it is of its nature
bound up with what today is known as an institution. Do not let
us be put off by this word. A community, even if its constituent
bonds are of a spiritual kind, cannot do without internal order
and a minimum of organisation. What we are going to discuss
is therefore religious life in so far as it is an institution.

First of all, we must have a clearly defined, common ideal:
we have to know what we are trying to do, we have to live the
ideal together, and to do this, we have to create certain living
conditions, yes, material ones. You only have to visit the little
old Franciscan friaries in Umbria or in the Vale of Rieti, to
see what sort of appropriate setting and atmosphere they create.
You can tell at once that these poor, humble, cheerful buildings
beautiful in their simplicity, formed an environment, the spirit
of which has seeped into their very stones. You sense that the
men who lived there, lived in a certain spirit, that they had
their rule, that they observed a way of living together, contributing to the creation of a new type of man with a very
definite type of spirituality. Here too, Brother Charles's hermitage—as he himself designed it—bears the imprint of his spirit
and helps to create its own unique atmosphere, even though the
surroundings are changing fast and things are not what they
were. Buildings are not of course the most important aspect of an
environment, though they are important all the same. People
today are learning this to their cost: in olden days, towns and
buildings had what you might call a human soul; the buildings
in the new towns of today do not. Brother Charles was aware of

this, and took great pains in the chapter of his rule dealing with Fraternity buildings to explain how much these 'will impress their character on the brothers'. Even man's most inward life is affected to some extent by his material surroundings. We could say a lot more about this, but we must go further with our analysis of the ideal environment for a religious community.

First we shall explain how this environment has to be quickened by a common soul, and we shall see what this is. Next, we shall see how this environment must afford a place for every member of the community, in a spirit of sharing and mutual consultation. Lastly, we shall have to understand how obedience, making Christ present among men, transforms a human community into an ecclesial community.

* * *

Of that first Christian community in Jerusalem, Scripture tells us that 'the whole group of believers was united, heart and soul'. These believers however were of widely differing origin and temperament. They had problems, and we should not gloss them over. None the less, they had one common soul and heart.

What made religious communities of the past—and what has made the Fraternity too—is that these communities found their soul, a living soul quickening everything, common to everyone. This soul is the principle of unity and communion between the members. This soul takes shape in a certain way of thinking and acting in common. It is the product of a spirituality, of an ideal, common to all and each, and of the willingness of all to help each other to bring it into being. What is wrecking some congregations today is that they are losing their common soul. This happens when they start questioning their aim and the means required to attain it.

Every type of religious life entails practising the precepts given by Jesus in the Gospel; each congregation does this according to its own spirit. A spirit is always hard to define; you might as well try to define a person. You may to some extent be able to describe his features and his character, but you cannot define him. A community is like a person, each with its own indefinable, unique spiritual personality. Hence the danger is trying to produce a photographic, or 'identikit', portrait of one. However much we may say about the religious life or about the Fraternity, will never exhaust what there is to be said, since a soul is not something that you can define: it is something you live, and something you encounter. And, I should add, this soul has been given to us by the Lord, and handed on by the Holy Spirit from generation to generation. So we receive it, but cannot fully define it. Were it of human origin, we might perhaps be able to draw up rules by which it could be completely defined. If we found a sports club, we can say quite positively what it is: aims, conditions of membership, rules, right down to the colour of the bathing trunks. But a religious community is a gift from God. It is founded on the flowering of a charism given to a founder. A congregation cannot spring into existence out of the blue: it has to spring from a seed implanted in the Church by the Holy Spirit, and this seed is something living and completely human, though as mysterious as life, indeed as the Life coming from on high. How the seed grows will of course depend on us. We have to make it grow, but we are not the ones who made it in the first place. What is more, we cannot make it. We must be very clear about this: the religious environment differs from a human environment in that, at its birth, a gift was made by God, whose gifts surpass anything that we ourselves might think of. Whenever the Council, whether in *Lumen Gentium* or in *Ecclesiae Sanctae*, mentions reforms or adaptations of the religious life, it always uses the word 'renewal', as though it meant reviving a wilting, or even dying, plant. And the Council adds that congregations should constantly refer back to the charism of their respective founders.

Our religious life is thus a gift from God, confided to our care, and we must guard it faithfully. For it is within our power to stifle it and destroy it, even though we are bidden constantly to make it new, to make it live, to renew it, to bring it back to life. When we manage to make a heart start beating again after it has stopped, we say that we have brought it back to life. But this can only happen because it is not quite dead in the first place. We may find ourselves in the same situation, sometimes, when we are responsible for our own community and for the gift of religious life entrusted to us by the Lord. For, sad as it is, we can just as easily let our ideal grow lifeless as we can put new life into it; we can also distort it, or corrupt it from within. If the distortion arises merely because of our limitations, because we are imperfect and cannot manage to live our ideal properly, this is not too serious, since God, knowing us and cherishing no illusions about us, has already foreseen all this. Not that I mean that we should lightly resign ourselves to distorting our ideal: but how can we help doing so? So long as we know, and are sorry about it, and are humble enough to keep trying to do better, that is enough. The motto for us when facing up to the ideal entrusted to us by the Lord should be: Always dare as much as you dare. We ought always to dare to the limit: and this holds good for all the contingencies of Christian life too. Whether it be the demands of justice or of love, of evangelism, of the apostolate, of giving ourselves to others, of self-sacrifice, in a word, of everything that the Lord demands of us, we must dare to the limit. We must always use up whatever grace avails at the moment.

More serious than the deficiencies in the way we live our ideal, is to allow our ideal to be corrupted. A terrible thing, indeed! Corruption sets in when we substitute human considerations for the promptings of the Holy Spirit: this means distorting the charism, destroying it from within. The common soul is, remember, the presence of Christ—for, as we have already seen, every form of religious life contains a call to make a total gift of ourselves to the Lord. He is there, in every community gathered in the name of Christ, to transform us, to make us more like him, not only by some outward way of life or even in very practical ways, but deep down in the core of our being. This transformation that we undergo is something very concrete, very personal, and this is why it takes all sorts of different forms. People often ask why there are so many different spiritual families in the Church. To which the answer quite simply is: because living people are involved. Could living beings, particularly when we are talking of so exalted a plane as the divine life, ever be standardised to conform to two or three types imposed by us on the living freedom of the Holy Spirit? A congregation quickened by a common soul has its own uniquely inimitable features. Any standardising of the religious life would tragically distort the features of Christ in his Church. It would also have grave effects for the individual religious themselves, obliged to conform to a limited number of stereotypes. You see, the Holy Spirit in its living interventions works on a grander scale than we do when we create things. Some systems of religious training have admittedly made the mistake of trying to turn out all their religious like identical plaster casts. But this is not at all the same thing as feeling that you belong to one same religious family. This does not abolish individual personality. If you look at the children in a family, you will find that they are all different, some diametrically so, but that they all have something in common: they make up a family, an environment of their own, a loving community. And so it is in a spiritual community, such as yours. You all have your share in a common soul, but God is aware that you are and will always be each of you different from the other, for the greater good, be it said, of the ideal to which you are dedicated, and which is to be put into practice in the Church.

Responsibility for this common soul then falls fully on all and each of you, in the sense that it cannot exist without your gift of yourself, of your brain, of your heart and—more important still—because you will love your Fraternity, love its ideal and love its soul. If you do not love your community, your Fraternity, you will not be able to draw life from it, and you will forthwith begin to be—whether you wish it or not—an element corrupting the ideal.

I said that we have to give our brain. Since what we are talking about is a charism, a gift of the Spirit, we must accept it in a spirit of total availability. This implies an attitude of faith with the humility and intelligence that such an attitude requires: for we receive the gift of our vocation from someone who is greater than we are, holier than we are, Jesus Christ. The common soul of our community has its foundations in the gift that each of us makes of him or herself to Jesus. This is how the spirit of brotherhood is born and grows.

*　*　*

The second element essential to a religious environment is its capacity to find a place for every member.

All human communities naturally tend to generate a kind of collectivism: what one might call community materialism. I am not saying that religious communities are becoming collectivist. But there is always a danger of this happening, once a community's aim ceases to be fixed on a reality higher than man, on putting the Gospel into practice or on imitating Christ. You see, when a community has a sufficiently lofty aim, this encourages the individual development of each community member: the aim, being higher than man, draws him upward. But when a community—a political party for example—sets itself a goal lower than man, let us say to create a prosperous economy, from that moment the danger of collectivism sets in, since people can be used as tools to attain an objective lower than man. And this can happen in a religious community too, and no less so for being more or less masked. As for instance, when a community dedicated to such and such a work becomes completely engrossed in the material aspects of doing this work, then, without even realising, that community has become enslaved to its work, to the exclusion of that higher aim of serving God. A kind of community materialism has already set in. Its members start being made use of for some thing, and this is the very negation of the divine environment quickened by Christ, which ought to be generated by every religious community. A community should not make use of its members; the members should serve the common good of the community —which is something quite different. A community should serve Christ and his Church.

The unity of the Fraternity comes from this unity of ideal and from the communion of hearts resulting from it. The willingness to find a place for each, which ought to characterise the community, is one of the most important fruits of brotherly love, a love informed by faith, be it said, a truly Christian love in the sense that its aim is that each shall belong entirely to Christ. This is what we should want and try to bring about for each one of us.

No easy undertaking, this, to walk—harbouring no illusions —straight into the thick of the difficulties inherent in community life. First of all, there are the personal problems. Sometimes we are inclined to dignify these into 'cases' (as the psychiatric term is) under the impression that these problems are uniquely ours. They usually arise from social relationships. But who is not a 'case'? At least, occasionally! And when you are living together, each wallowing in the misery of his own particular problems, so that the Fraternity becomes the aggregate, the common pool, of everybody's problems, how intolerable that would be! How depressing the atmosphere of a community engrossed in the personal hang-ups and problems of its members!

It would be right to say that a community's unity, a community's soul, is not primarily the product of what its members are at the moment, nor of the qualities or gifts that they possess. For then unity would imply that we all had the same gifts and the same needs: like a photographic club or a sports club, drawing its unity and cohesion from what each member has in common with the others, such as wanting to learn about photography, or to play football. Here the members pool what they have in common and this unites them. But in the case of a Christian or of a religious community, what unites the members does not even exist yet, it is something still to be. The goal is what they have in common: to become more and more like Christ in a given spiritual climate and spiritual family: a hope stretching away into the future. So, in our case, what unites us is rather what we have not yet got, something we stretch out for, something we lack and which we know we cannot get without the help of others. The common enterprise before us is what unites us, even if we are not all likely to accomplish it in the same way. What unites us most closely is what lies ahead of us, the goal—more than what we ourselves are, since we are different from each other in so many ways, sometimes even diametrically so. We all have different temperaments, come from different backgrounds and different countries, have different ways of speaking, and we each have our own different problems. Yet we all want the same thing, the same ideal. The Lord wants to perform the same transforming work in each of us, although this transformation will be uniquely individual to each. We know very well that we cannot achieve this transformation on our own. Hence what unites us is what still has to be done.

If we were really to grasp this, how it would widen our horizons and make our community-hope take on more positive shape! Oh yes, a community is like a person: you can talk about a community's faith, its hope, its love. We should always be trying to develop our community's hope: that is, our common effort to help one another to achieve our ideal. But to do this, we must acquire a readiness to accept the next man, which we so often lack! Of course it is an obstacle, but we have to keep on learning to overcome it. Each member should be able to feel that he is fully accepted and understood as he is, by each of his brothers, above all by his superiors, and hence by the whole community. The Fraternity should be characterised by the feeling that each member truly belongs. Each should feel at ease in it, knowing himself accepted for himself and understood as he is.

The first condition for this willingness to accept one another is the conviction that we cannot attain the goal for which we entered the Fraternity without helping each other. We can only fulfil our vocation together, such is the law of Christianity. If we develop this attitude of accepting and respecting our brothers by doing our best to help them to give of their best, then the community will be truly fulfilling its Christian function; this is what Christ has always wanted and we shall ourselves experience his joy.

If a community is to fulfil this ideal, it must not concentrate on a material goal. It must concentrate on a spiritual one, which must be Christ himself—no less—to whom we owe the gift of our lives. More concretely, the community must fulfil the conditions of the Kingdom taught by Jesus. I have already spoken of these conditions, and they have to be very concrete. Everything matters in an environment for living, in a community, since we are poor things needing favourable living conditions, even lowly material ones. We need a climate, a setting, we need things to create an atmosphere. Every community expresses itself in its own customs, in its own ways of doing things—such as you would find in any family. This is what helps to make a unique 'personalised' atmosphere. It is wrong to think that a religious can live outside his community or that he can do without it. It is sometimes claimed that the need of the religious for an environment, for a truly accepting community, indicates a sort of withdrawal, a refusal to take risks. You hear people talk of 'taking refuge in a community'—like the cities of refuge in ancient times. Secularisation tends to make a religious live among men, alone, virtually cut off from community life. This is an impossible situation; a cruel one too, since everyone has a right to his proper environment. It is also contrary to Christianity with its tendency to express itself in communities.

So we can say quite emphatically that the Fraternity is to be your natural environment, where you know that you can develop as your vocation requires: an environment which you cannot do without, even if it should happen, for legitimate reasons, that you have to leave it from time to time. If you think that you can be faithful to your vocation without the support of the Fraternity, you are wrong. You may be tempted to think so because the common life, whatever its joys may be, very often seems a hard road and on occasion a heavy cross, particularly for some temperaments. And then we begin to put too human a construction on our ideal of 'self-fulfilment'. This is a problem that we often run into, when thinking about community life today.

We have a right to feel accepted by our brothers, yes, and to be understood and deeply respected by them too: but this does not mean that we should assume the whole community to be at our beck and call to do what we want and to give us everything we need, as we ourselves may judge, for our own 'self-fulfilment'. The word is thoroughly overworked today, and is horribly ambiguous. We should remember that he who exclusively seeks his own fulfilment, will never find it. He who in abnegation gives up seeking it, will be the one to find it. Christ himself warned us of this: 'Anyone who loses his life for my sake will find it.' If you want to preserve your life, you will look on everything in terms of your own self-fulfilment, you will make yourself incapable of that true fulfilment promised in the Gospel.

All the same, we have to recognise that we often encounter a real difficulty here: not everyone is yet capable of the fulfilment promised in the Gospel. We have to remember than man is like a frail plant or a weak animal; he has to go through various stages of development, particularly those of childhood and adolescence, during which he feels a vital need for a certain range of living conditions which he does not always get. Freedom to renounce oneself comes later, as the fruit of maturity. Things are often made more complicated than they need be. Certainly, there are some people who have such and such an emotional need, some need for fulfilment, so essentially part of their nature that it cannot be overridden without producing damaging frustrations. The human organism is nothing if not complex. And you can see how our spiritual development, with its infinitely high objective, is likely to run into all kinds of obstacles, none of them easy to overcome, since they do not necessarily depend on our own will. In these special cases, the community spirit of acceptance is a great help.

What we are saying now, however, is for those brothers and sisters who are capable of renouncing themselves, of hearing the word of Christ and his call to renunciation. If you do not feel yourself ready for this, perhaps you should consider waiting for a while: everything depends on your stage of development. If you are capable of sacrifice, of forgetting yourself for the sake of others, in a word, of losing your life by giving it, then you may come in—enter the religious life. If not, you need more preparation. Of course, situations are not always quite as clear-cut as that. We shall always have residual problems—each of us—but it does not do to take too much notice of them. I repeat, the community is not at your beck and call. The community may have a duty to accept you, but you have the duty of serving it. The serving cannot be all one way: you will serve the community and avoid making use of it by learning to accept your brothers or your sisters. And this is where, of course, we often become discouragingly aware of our own limitations, and of other people's limitations too. There will be moments of exasperation, conflicts of character, incompatibilities of temperament. This is perfectly normal; we have to accept that we are only human. Over-idealising is as harmful as rejecting an ideal. It is an excess, producing its own crop of illusions and errors. It can even be erected into a system, a view of life in which imperfections are deliberately ignored, a rejection of reality therefore, and hence in the ultimate analysis a rejection of the laws governing the normal development of our spiritual nature and of our emotions. Then we are tempted to isolate ourself and feel the lure of solitude; we are in fact being tempted to withdraw from the community. We must analyse these feelings when they come, since the community, like the brotherly life, entails crosses and the claims of discipline. Sometimes, we may feel like running away. A favourable religious environment ought to be loved. We must pay great attention to this, for the environment can become unbearably burdensome, whereas it ought to be something that sets us free.

All the same, the common life should certainly admit times for relaxation, allowing periods of solitude with God alone. The polarities of Christian life, which we talked about at the outset, of achieving intense communion with men, and of pursuing an ever closer intimacy with God, have each their proper claims. We shall come back to this when we talk about prayer. Meanwhile, I should like to make the point that it is also one of the functions of the religious environment to provide times of absolute silence, leisure-times for prayer, times for solitude with God. The community ought to make solitude with God possible. If it does not, it will not be a Christ-like community, and will not be a favourable religious environment.

*   *   *

And now I come to the third aspect of this environment: which is that it should be favourable to sharing and mutual consultation. If every community should have its own common soul and common goal, this means that each and every member is totally and constantly responsible for achieving this. It therefore follows, if we are to help each other, that the way to achieve this common soul entails sharing and mutual consultation. I shall call this the common search for the best. There is no need to labour the point, since it is in tune with contemporary trends. But it does require a little study to see it in its true perspective: it too makes stern demands.

The search is not only concerned with the common good, but also with what is better and best for each. For we do not live as individuals in the community, but as people each of whom has his own good to seek and to be sought by all the others. The search will also be concerned with the best conditions for evangelistic work or even the best environment for the Fraternity; things that have to be constantly rethought, if they are to be improved.

I need hardly point out that the common search entails risks, like everything else. The risks are: endless discussion, refusal to budge from one's point of view, and the substituting of unproductive chatter for meditative enquiry. In larger communities especially, mutual consultation can give rise to pressure groups, that is, minorities seeking to impose their own ideas by means sometimes far from democratic, and not scrupling to impose them by adopting techniques of group-psychology, irrespective of their brothers' opinions and freedom of choice. This can indeed happen, though I am glad to say that it has not yet happened in our Fraternity. But I do know congregations that have been completely ruined by such proceedings. The activity of the Spirit is, so to speak, so closely identified with the activity of man, and with his faculties of thinking freely and acting freely, that every type of society, even ecclesial and religious, is subject to the laws normally governing consultative meetings, and is all the more likely to get stuck at the ordinary human level, the more numerous its members are and the less aware how faith and love should guide and inform their mutual relationships within the community. All common search therefore should be conducted in a spirit of faith and in openness to the original charism, and not in terms of a fancied charismatic spirit which we may think fit to attribute to ourselves.

The spirit of sharing in mutual respect and confidence, and the common pursuit of the congregation's goal, are enjoying a genuine renewal today, but are not something new in the Church. These have been wholeheartedly practised since her earliest centuries and from the outset of every type of religious order. The old authors called it having spiritual goods in common, and saw it as the very seed of the true spirit of poverty. They said: 'If between brothers and sisters in religion we pool our spiritual goods, why not also pool our material possessions?'. The sharing of material possessions they saw as the consequence, the outward expression and sign of a deeper sharing. Without the latter, the sharing of material possessions would have struck them as a dead sort of poverty, as a form without content.

Yes, the sharing of material possessions should be the sign of a deeper sharing, I mean the common soul of the Fraternity. You understand that doing this is very exacting. But this is what Christ offers to those who wish to be his close followers. And this is why he requires of us, his disciples, a humble heart and an ear readily attentive to his word: comparing this to the simplicity of little children. These are the dispositions that we must have in our mutual consultation, since without a humble heart and spirit we cannot attain true respect for our brothers. The habit of sharing everything and of marching together makes the common soul of the Fraternity, of each fraternity, and that soul is the fruit of a genuine brotherly love and not just a matter of words.

Good intentions and loving hearts do not in themselves create an atmosphere of acceptance in a fraternity: there must be human cordiality and joy. It must be positive. Chastity and spiritualised love must not be allowed to knock the heart out of it, if you follow me. Everything that is pure, true, great in human friendship must be safeguarded. There is no need at all for a religious community to secrete a chilling atmosphere of insensitivity and indifference: this is a false austerity. But a true, joyous austerity—that we cannot do without. And I do not mean an atmosphere of nonchalance shot through with ill-controlled emotion. That is quite different. A climate embued with a common soul, with an undivided heart, having and sharing all spiritual goods in common, should itself generate that joy which is the fruit of love. This joy does not prevent us from experiencing troubles, it does not abolish the causes of hurt and suffering, it does not dispense us from the Cross: but it does make them all fruitful. It is the source of deep peace; it develops that feeling of security, when each man knows that he is truly supported, helped and watched over by his brothers. And this is why the tendency to avoid sharing and having all things in common is such a threat to the life of a religious community.

These are some of the elements essential to the common life as led by religious. I have spoken about environment, and once again I must emphasise the importance of this. You might say that it stands for those aspects of the common life creating favourable conditions for each member to advance towards perfection, while alone creating the conditions which make it possible for us to lead the chaste, poor and obedient life held up to us by Christ, expected of us by the Church, needed of us by our brothers—barely to mention these to whose destiny the inscrutable designs of Providence have linked us in our mission as evangelists.

4
Obedience and Freedom in Christ

WE HAVE BEEN talking about the brotherly community and how it forms the right and indispensable environment for every religious, and we have also seen how sharing everything is, as it were, the material aspect of communion with our brothers—a communion with our brothers to be intensified and divinised by Christ until it forms a strict bond between the community and him; for the Church is the Body of Christ: she is Christ. And a religious community is also Christ.

Now we must talk about a characteristic which is essential to a community becoming Christ. I mean, obedience. Obedience makes Christ present at the level of the community, and thus transforms a human into an ecclesial community. Obedience is therefore very important. The Church, in so far as it is a human society, remains subject to all the laws of a human society. And when we are dealing with a community, by the same token, we must always be realistic and pay great attention to what will make it work properly; you cannot put a community together in a haphazard way. There is, however, in every ecclesial community a dimension which is truly supernatural and therefore not strictly amenable to the planner. And this dimension is obedience in Christ. For obedience resides in love, obedience leads us into Christ. Christ unites us in his love; the first commandment, which he made his own, is that we should love one another as he has loved us; and within this revelation of the love that God bears for us, we discover obedience in its purest form, since obedience is the highest form of love. Christ loved, and because he loved, he made himself obedient, even to accepting death, death on a cross. Obedience being so closely bound to love, we shall have to consider it in those two dimensions of the mystery of Christ expressed in the twin polarities of the Gospel, which I keep mentioning: extremely intimate communion with God and an equally intimate communion with our brothers. Obedience is going to manifest itself in these two directions.

When we talk of communion with our brothers, we have to recall the concept of the brotherly society in which this communion comes about. There is no need to over-emphasise the demands that this society makes: no society can exist without laws or without authority. However simple you make it, however brotherly it may be, it cannot do without laws and authority. No society can exist without them. Even the most spontaneous types are subject to these basic needs. And often the spontaneous ones are the most authoritarian of all, since they crystallise round one forceful personality: as you may see with gangs of adolescents. Every society is articulated by an authority and by laws; were it not so, you would have an anonymous crowd or incoherent mass. Anarchy, far from what many people think, is just what does not make people happy or allow them to fulfil themselves. An anarchic society does not let people develop normally.

Of course, the way that authority is exercised and the way that the laws are applied, can give rise to every imaginable excess and abuse, since man seeks his freedom and this is hard to find. A man who assumes the responsibilities of government is also seeking his freedom, but remains enslaved to his ambition, passions, temperament or, despite his good intentions, remains a prisoner of his own imperfect and limited ideals; he is also trapped in the limitations of his own knowledge and of the facts at his disposal. It is always hard to admit that laws are made to safeguard our freedom, and not to enslave us.

A society does not exist for the sake of existing but for some goal, and it thus has its own good. The Fraternity's reason for existing is to make you into true Little Brothers; it also has a mission in the Church: it has a personality, which is expressed in a whole range of things that would be difficult to define and which we call the common good. This comprehends the ideal pursued and also everything needful to the fulfilment of each member of the community for the putting of this ideal into effect. I use the word fulfilment in its fullest, truest sense. The common good of the Fraternity extends also to the evangelistic work to which we are dedicated, and to the activities required of us in this context. And lastly, it is an expression of that holiness which Christ wishes to reveal through the community, set as a sign in the midst of human society. You see what a complex thing this common good is. It is not only an ideal, but really a life to be lived, always new, according to changing conditions of time and place, to be lived in a concrete, practical way. Undertakings like this cannot proceed without their troubles, mistakes and fumblings, not without careful thought. And finally, there is this attentiveness to the Holy Spirit, constantly breathing new life into our little society by virtue of its relationship to the Church, from which it receives its life-force as the branch does from the vine. The Holy Spirit is at work in the Church, the Holy Spirit is at work in every heart; there is no contradiction between any of his countless activities, only perfect harmony.

We are each of us responsible for this complex, ever-present, common good. And this is why—and I cannot stress this too much—from the moment you want to accept all the consequences of joining the Fraternity, you as a member of the Church become the servant of the common good and must be willing to feel responsible for it. Being responsible for the common good and knowing what it is are the building blocks of any religious community. Otherwise, it would never be more than a collection of individuals asking a religious organisation to supply them with services. When the members of a community only look on it as a range of common services for board and lodging, intellectual work or some other well-defined activity, clearly that community has ceased to be one. At any rate, it is no longer a religious community. It is only a body—there is no soul. Of course, every community does tend by force of entropy to degenerate in this direction, such being the imperfections and limitations inherent in all human institutions; but we must constantly be fighting against this.

And now we come to the question of authority and how it relates to the freedom of each member. For, if all the members

of the community ought to have a sense of personal responsibility for the common good, they ought by the same token to
submit to an authority. In the course of history, authority has
been wielded in all manner of ways in the Church and in the
religious life, adopting many different systems of government.
Today, we are moving towards a new conception of government, in religious life as in political life, both of these being
affected by the psychological changes undergone by man himself, his political maturity, and his growing awareness of being
responsible for his environment. It is therefore natural and even
desirable that religious should be more aware of their responsibilities as regards the whole apparatus of their Order or
Congregation. We must, however, strike a balance between the
inner and outward law in the religious life. A community may
bind its members by any number of positive and detailed regulations, to show them the right path to follow. But to be realistic,
you can only lay down a few broad lines of conduct and rely
on the inner law, that is, on the fact that each member has a
sufficiently instructed, vigorous and enlightened conscience, for
him to make the right decisions for himself. Between outward
law and the law of conscience should be a constant equilibrium,
and this requires tact, delicacy of touch, and knowledge of the
human heart with all its needs and weaknesses.

The last Council had a great deal to say about freedom,
especially in the religious life. Today, we like looking back to
what happened at the birth of that first Christian community to
throw off the shackles of the Law—not, as some people think,
of the Divine Law, but of the Mosaic Law with its top-heavy
superstructure of ritual regulations. This was true liberation for
the children of God; Christ had so developed their conscience—
the inner law of that first Christian community—had so imprinted his spirit on it, that there was no further need for them
to be bound by the innumerable prescriptions of the Law. The
demands of the Divine Law over against those of the host of
prescriptions of the Mosaic Law were frequently alluded to by
Christ in his discussions with the Pharisees and Doctors of the
Law: 'You have made God's word null and void by means of
your Traditions.' The present trend in religious life is to in-
crease the role of the inner law and correspondingly to diminish
that of the outward law. And since this is all to the good—the

common as well as the individual good—it indicates a further ripening of the individual conscience, as also of our sense of responsibility for our own and our brothers' religious life.

This more responsible attitude should not produce a less obedient one, but it does alter the respective roles played by personal conscience and the inner law on the one hand, and by the obligations of the community rule on the other. When we talk about perfect obedience, we must not confuse the quality and intensity of personal commitment required, with what might be called its quantity or diffusion. Christ obeyed more perfectly than any man can obey. He obeyed the essence of his Father's will, and this led him to the Cross. Christ did not perform a gamut of acts of obedience, but one act of such a nature and quality as to embrace his whole life.

When Christ created his Church, he used the raw material of human society with its natural needs for government and organisation, for authority and law. Of this society he made his Church: a divinised society of which he himself is soul and Head; in which all authority derives from him; a society having the same aim as his own when he made himself obedient even to death on a cross, that is to say, the redemption of mankind and the liberation of our souls. And this too is the purpose and meaning of authority in the religious life. So, ever since then, there has been this invisible fact, accessible only to the eye of faith. And when people try to treat the ecclesial society as you might any other society, subjecting its government and organisation to rational analysis in exclusively human terms, it is rather like conducting an autopsy on someone after killing him: all you have left is a corpse. When they subject a religious community—with its ecclesial authority and its vow of obedience uniting the members to their community—to exclusively rational analysis, they forget that the object of their analysis is mysteriously united to the living Christ.

We certainly ought to have a healthily critical approach to the way we live in community; we must be ready to discuss it, so that we can do better. We should always be guided by reason. But criticism must be illuminated by faith. If religious obedience strikes people as being out of date, the reason is that they are not making their judgments in the light of faith. I do not mean abuses of authority, or mistaken notions, or too narrow interpretations of obedience, but the principle itself. Religious obedience will always be a mystery of faith, inaccessible to those who lack the simplicity of heart and mind to accept the Kingdom of God as Jesus intends us to accept it.

Full acceptance of the mystery of obedience is indispensable to the forming of a brotherly community. You see, we cannot attain the intimate communion that religious life ought to achieve between us, unless we pass by way of intimate communion with God on the Cross of Christ. The ecclesial community entails qualities that can only come through obedience. Obedience therefore helps to make us free, helps towards our redemption. And again, the Fraternity is more than an ordinary human society, since it partakes of that union which is between Christ and his Church.

Among the somewhat contradictory aspirations affecting the world today, several arouse sympathetic echoes in religious congregations and give rise to problems that we shall now have to consider. There is, for instance, a tendency to cry down the importance of congregational unity, in favour of developing the national or regional character of the religious foundations in any given country. This is regarded as a proper result of cultural assimilation. But it has its drawbacks. Acceptable as it may be as a corrective to excessive uniformity in religious life dependent on a single point of view, there is a risk here of negating one of the characteristics of the Kingdom of God: which is to transcend all cultures and unite the People of God as brothers without regard to frontier or race. In any case, this need for unity is spontaneously, often violently, experienced by young people today. We have been gathered out of every race and every nation, into the unity of Christ, and have been offered to the Lamb. Every ecclesial community, and more so every religious community, is called to put this vision of universality into practice, as an earnest of the Kingdom in which there is no more Jew, Greek, Roman or pagan; we should beware of thwarting the Kingdom's growth in love and mutual understanding for the sake of cultural values which in any case are relative and sometimes open to question.

On the score of renewal and adaptation, congregational unity can also be undermined at another level. Some institutes have thought fit to split into different language-groups. These reforms have been motivated by unduly rational, where not actually political, considerations. In certain cases, admittedly, the idea has been to show increased respect for a cultural or national identity, which perhaps has been repressed or oppressed in the past; and to give it a better chance of making its own contribution to the Universal Church. This too is very good, but again we must be sure not to let a reform of this sort conflict with something more important still in Christ's teaching. Where cultures have been shabbily treated, where there has been more or less intentional oppression, we should try to put this behind us and rise above it. Unity is not the same thing as uniformity. And the tendency to confuse centralisation and uniformity with unity has done much harm in the Church. It has caused schisms which might have been avoided; it gave rise to the mutual misunderstanding separating East from West; whereas the seemingly irreconcilable principles at stake might have been able to witness to two complementary and equally important aspects of one united Church. Here, history shows how weak man is, how ill equipped to rise above his limitations: we fumble about, stressing first one thing, then another, but even so, we ought at least to be aware of the direction in which we should be going.

We, for our part, sons and daughters of the 'little universal brother', rather than devalue our ideal or, worse, frustrate the purpose for which Christ died, must never, never stop trying to become more and more united in one single great community, founded on mutual respect and understanding in Love. This gathering of all in unity—different as you are from one another—is one of the Fraternity's essential tasks. We cannot stop striving for this without failing in our vocation.

In practice, however, how is this to be achieved, given that you are not all always likely to agree when it comes to assessing situations, having ideas, making plans and taking decisions? Unity is lost before even glimpsed, unless centred on a higher good, proffered equally through obedience to every man and every woman called by the Church in Christ's name to bring this unity into being at the price of renouncing his or her own will.

No easy undertaking, this. It requires courage and determination in faith. For we shall often find ourselves faced with painful situations. And superiors, being men like ourselves, will always have their faults. Each has his own temperament and his own limitations. And it will sometimes happen that the final decision taken by our superior does not seem the best one to us. And here you come up against a very common case of conscience today: the conflict between the judgment of my own conscience and a decision made by the Church or by my superior. My conscience, obliging me to do what I judge to be best, forbids me to obey the order that I have received. That is the objection. We must reduce this to its proper proportions.

A superior's decision is nearly always concerned with practical matters. His decisions hardly ever affect matters of principle; and these in any case are usually clearly defined in our constitutions. If the superior's point of view is only relative, yours is only relative too. Who is to judge between you? And even supposing your own view to be more correct than his, the fact that you disobey him would cause you and the community far more harm than any that might result from your carrying out an order that you consider mistaken or second best. Every act of disobedience inflicts a wound on the common good: you harm your community and your brothers. Even in trivial matters, disobedience, if really such, causes some harm; whereas the harm flowing from an error of judgment on the part of your superior is far from certain, and in any case can nearly always be put right. Bear this in mind, and remember your responsibility for the common good of the Fraternity, and for the common good of your brothers or your sisters. Disobedience is catching, causes ruin in the hearts, destroys, does not build up. Once we have agreed to bind ourselves to a community for life, for better for worse, for joy and for tribulation, because we know that this is what the Lord expects of us, and that this community is where we are going to fulfil our lives, our missions in the Church, and where we shall truly belong to the Lord: and know that the Fraternity is to be the way of perfection for us; then, we have to accept the consequences and bear the responsibilities that this entails. And our responsibility is to obey, with true and sometimes painful obedience, painful as the cross on which Christ himself obeyed.

This leads us to another question: whether it is possible to strive after Christ-like perfection and give ourselves to Christ, without being often forced to make painful sacrifices? When we make our profession, we commit ourselves concretely to a life of chastity, poverty and obedience. But this is only the outward expression of a much deeper commitment, entailing our giving our entire selves to Jesus and his Father. By profession, we give ourselves without reservation, we dedicate ourselves to God. Jesus accepts our gift. He accepts us through the medium of his Church, since we make our profession with our hands in the Church's hands; but we also dedicate ourselves to the community of our brothers or our sisters. The community too receives our profession, and this binds us to all our brothers: and from that moment we are responsible for them, just as they are responsible for us. To some degree, we put our lives in the hands of our superior and of the community, since superiors are part of that community and represent it. As in the Church our profession binds us not only to her pastors, but to all the faithful, to the whole assembly of the People of God, in which each of us receives his own task, or mission, or ministry; so in the Fraternity, being that part of the Church which accepts us, to which we give ourselves and which takes responsibility for us, but for which we too must accept responsibility, with all that this entails. This is why the act of profession is so far-reaching in its effects. Profession is far from being of purely personal consequence.

We have said enough to show what an indispensable element obedience is to a brotherly religious community and to the environment that this represents for us. We could go on to talk about the difficulties of obedience, and of its fruits too; I shall not do so, since you know that already. Obedience, does, however, lead us on to another important aspect of the religious life which we shall now consider: the mystery of the Cross.

* * *

The purpose of baptism and of the whole Christian life is to set us free. This particular aspect of the Christian vocation has never seemed more important than now, when the People of God seem to be clamouring for it all the time. We claim to be free, with the freedom of the children of God. But what does this really mean? No one really knows, and freedom is such a

vague term, rather like love, covering a whole variety of feelings, sometimes virtually contradictory. Christ made himself
obedient, even to accepting death, death on a cross, to set us
free from sin and its effects: this is what salvation means. We
are set free from sin by the gift of eternal life. Why? Because
God is holy and—here we touch on another mystery—man in
his turn must also become holy. This idea that man must be
holy because God is holy may also seem out of date. Hence the
temptation to adapt the concept of holiness to contemporary
thinking by presenting it as the effect of man's being set free
from all oppression by a process of socio-political evolution. We
cannot tackle this subject now, but there is a real problem
here, and one not easily solved. The solution, however, depends
on the view we take of the relationship between the building of
the Kingdom of God on earth and the various evolutionary and
political notions of liberation. Ours is, to concentrate here on
salvation in Christ, with its effects on our religious and community life.

I need hardly remind you that in fact we are not free, or
more exactly, we are not yet free. We have to accept this, if we
want to understand the true nature of the liberation for which
we thirst. We are not free, even though we often think we are.
In fact, man is enslaved in all sorts of almost inescapable ways,
some inward, some outward. We are dependent on, indeed
prisoners of, our environment and of various sorts of conditioning affecting all human life. There is much truth in the
Marxist assertion that man is shaped, entirely conditioned, by
the economic environment in which he lives. But dependence
on the environment, in certain ways good and necessary, is also
a form of slavery. Accepting that man be conditioned by his
economic and material environments (which are in themselves
inferior to the dignity of his nature) means denying the dignity
of man, since this consists precisely in his being able, by the
exercise of freewill, to dominate everything inferior to himself,
and to submit to God alone. This is what true freedom is. Man,
king of creation and lord of all things, ceases to be so once he
becomes enslaved by them.

As for inner slavery, a little self-knowledge tells us how many
forms this can take! First, the slavery of ignorance on matters of
basic importance to us: we are ignorant about God, and even

about our own nature. Centuries of thought have not dispelled our ignorance here. Each new generation is as benighted as the last. We are ignorant about other people: how hard it is to know someone, our brother, however close! Not only do we not know him, but our attitude towards him is coloured by prejudice, hasty judgment and pre-conceived ideas. We may often think that there is nothing to be done about this: we are imprisoned in our inability to know, and cannot get out. We are also slaves to our imagination, which raises all sorts of problems, dangers and delusions; and are afraid. We are afraid of the future, afraid of what is hard and exacting, we are afraid of giving ourselves. Fear is the daughter of imagination, not of truth. And then, worst of all, there is the weakness of our will, caused in great part by all these various forms of enslavement. And, finally, there is the slavery of our psycho-physical make-up, what you might call the drag of the body with its imperious needs: sleep, the slowing-down of physiological function; the laws of nature; the disorderly impulses of sexuality, which can lead to a debasement and devaluation of love, and to the quest for sexual pleasure in dissociation from it. Passions rage: we cannot always control them. Then there is the unconscious mind, with its crop of complexes and even compulsions to crime. Tyrannical habits enslave us too and we keep contracting new ones. Even the apparently harmless ones, like drinking and smoking, are still forms of enslavement unworthy of human beings. And there are others, less evident perhaps but much deeper-rooted. We have not got much to be proud of in all this.

Christians, however, go on glibly telling the world that they are free, claiming to have thrown off those very laws, the observance of which ensures our inner freedom. Freedom, for a lot of people, means doing as they please, rejecting any form of constraint from outside, and letting spontaneity be their guide. Usually, this sort of behaviour does not in fact proceed from free decisions prompted by the Spirit, but from casual reaction to the environment and to the circumstances of the moment. We react, in point of fact, consistently with previous habit, out of ignorance, likes and dislikes, passion, desire for instant gratification: this is too often called freedom.

This is not the kind of freedom that we read about in the Gospel. This is not the freedom that Christ came to bring us and that the Church offers us as the reward of renunciation. That is something quite different. What Christ by his grace has put within our reach is the strength and power gradually to set ourselves free from sin and enslavement to evil, whether it be from within or from without. He who is truly free like this cannot be enslaved by anything on earth: he has become the slave of Christ. As St Paul proclaims: 'Nothing can come between us and the love of Christ.' If I belong to Christ, having reconquered my inner freedom in him, I need fear no further enslavement. Authority? Let them command me to do this or that, obedience makes me free. Throw me into prison, I am still free, Christian freedom finds its highest expression in martyrdom, that is to say, under violence, in the total negation of our most natural instinct for survival. To become capable of being 'obedient, even to accepting death, death on a cross', is the highest form of freedom for a Christian.

It is disconcerting, however, in daily life to find that baptised people are almost indistinguishable from unbaptised ones. You see, this freedom is not something handed to us ready-made. It is not already achieved in us by Christ's victory over evil. It is easy to make the mistake of thinking that it is. But in fact it is very hard for us to conquer our freedom. Every Christian is faced with this as his essential task on earth. In the catechism that our forefathers used to learn, the first question ran: 'Why did God make you?' To which the answer was: 'God made me to know Him and serve Him in this world, and to be happy with Him forever in the next.' Today perhaps such formulae make us smile; they have a flavour of 'individual' salvation, of which we no longer approve. I say 'perhaps'! For this answer is still basically correct. Isn't it in fact the right answer to our quest for the meaning of life, of life on earth, so brief yet so full of problems? Aren't we here to fulfil our destiny, and isn't that destiny to be made one with Christ? And how are we to become one with Christ, if we are not changed? The transformation of self does not mean living without laws, or as the times or cultural environment may dictate, but by discovering the true law of our own nature. And this law is the law of the Spirit, of which no one has ever written more lucidly or more forcefully than the apostle Paul. In his letters, we find a wonderfully complete exposition of the spiritual life. You can never read these too often. In them, St Paul, with all the vigour of a temperament brimming with vitality, tells us of his own experience; and this should carry great weight with us, for Paul had seen Christ, had understood Christ, had been captured by Christ and had given himself without reservation to Christ. But do not suppose that having seen Christ, Paul was not to have problems. Quite the reverse, he had very grave ones and had to keep up a furious struggle all along the line. He was a man of strong emotion; he had very fixed ideas: pupil of Gamaliel and zealous Pharisee, he had persecuted the Christians with all his zeal. And once he discovered Christ, he gave himself up whole-heartedly to the transformation being worked in him by the Master's grace—not without much soul searching and inner conflict. Here we see the true greatness of man; you do not come to this by easy ways.

If you come to the religious life with an ideal limited to your own opinions, without high ambitions, and without a readiness to grasp whatever the Lord expects of you, you would be wiser not to enter it. If you want to argue, to pare obedience down to the minimum, to make renunciation of the world as light a thing as you can; if you want to play at poverty, or insist on your own point of view in brotherly life as in evangelism; if you like doing as little as possible and mean to flee the spiritual combat; then you will certainly be unhappy, you will harm your brothers, and you would do better to go away, since your attitude would be a total contradiction of the life that you have chosen. Entering the religious life is choosing to obey the law of the Spirit, the law of Christ, an energetic law. Christ has never taught us easy things, he never makes minimal demands, and these may often seem harsh and even ruthless.

What causes so much harm today is that people are no longer quite sure what man is! To understand the effort that Jesus demands of us, and to understand the meaning of living by the Spirit, we must understand what we ourselves are. And indeed, we have to start living by the law of the Spirit before we can understand. There was, in the last century, a school of spirituality which used to present a view of life and man, in terms that we today regard as dualistic. The antagonists in the spiritual combat were carnal nature on the one hand and the life of the spirit on the other, hence the antithesis between the body as source of evil, and the soul as good element. The soul was thought of as being more or less imprisoned in the body, only escaping to freedom through death. Hence, a pessimistic view of man, whose true 'home' was in heaven and who meanwhile had to live his earthly, carnal days 'in exile'. From this to the notion that man was a 'spoiled' creature, was but a short step. This notion, widespread in the nineteenth century, as also in the Middle Ages, tended to minimise the reality of the world and its reasons for existing. Though it may have been a somewhat lopsided view of man, we cannot deny that the systems of spirituality based on it, produced saints, men and women remarkable for their human qualities none the less, living in obedience to the Spirit. Today we are coming back to a more biblical concept of man as a 'single reality'. We need not delve into the theoretical aspects of this. Suffice it to say that we are faced with a reality, with the enigma of man, and that the best way we can solve it is by obeying the law of the Gospel. For, man must either accept a law, a code of conduct from his God, and keep it, to fulfil himself and become truly man and son of God; or try himself to lay down a law for his own development, ultimately reducing himself to the dimensions seemingly indicated by reason and science. These are the alternatives: you have Marxist man, defined by reason in accordance with one view of the universe. Other philosophies propose other types. But for us Christians, Jesus Christ alone is the answer to the question: what is man and what should he become? For us, Jesus Christ is Man preeminent. This is why the saints, in the directness of their faith and without recourse to any other theory of man or, like Brother Charles, going beyond whatever philosophy had to say on the matter, simply decided that the time for arguing was over and that the time had come for giving themselves to Christ and obeying him. And we, by imitating them in taking the law of the Gospel as the true and joyous norm of human development, are certain of becoming as great and perfect as a man can and ought to be. Such is the choice we have to make. And of course, in making it, we are likely to run counter to what many people think we should be doing. If, however, we intend to follow the path of Jesus Christ, to follow the way of religious dedication, if we want to be real evangelists, if we want to learn how to pray, to become contemplatives, we have to follow the law of the Gospel unquestioningly, even if it does seem to conflict with views currently approved.

What God reveals to us through the lives of the saints is also very instructive for us. Here we are not likely to be mistaken, since we are no longer concerned with theories but with human successes. When a man makes a success of his life by making it really and truly an imitation of Christ, so that this success, call it holiness, shines out and irradiates others in their turn, there cannot be a mistake. Admittedly, we may interpret their lives in different ways, the types of spirituality themselves may vary, but once there is obedience to Christ, there is no mistake.

So there is this choice between two conceptions of man. If we choose Jesus Christ's conception of man, we have to admit that man has a spiritual law within him. And if there is such a thing as a spiritual law, does not this postulate the real existence of the spirit? The question is more serious than you might think. For if the spirit does not actually exist, but is only a figment of man's imagination, man's loneliness in the cosmos is truly appalling and what happens to us when we die cannot matter very much. Whether there is a future life or not, whether angels exist or not: all this becomes irrelevant, let alone how the fallen angels spend their time. What can it matter to us whether there are other-worldly beings or not, since they are inaccessible to us in any case? Meanwhile, here we are on earth, we have a job to do and we are equipped to do it: we can conquer the objective universe and plan the future of our race.

Refusal to face up to this question of where we are going has a marked effect on the way people live their lives today. On how you answer the question depends the 'meaning' you give to life, and your awareness of the laws that should govern it. Many people seem to be searching in the void, since they no longer know what to rely on in their quest for the true inner law of human development and human conduct. The uncertainty of the quest leads them into many a dead end.

We should do well to remember that there are different levels in human nature. There is, as it were on the surface of our being, the level of the senses, linking us to the external world. In depth, this level overlaps to some extent with the spirit, and flows into the level of the emotions and the realm of feelings. All very complicated, to be sure. Then there is the level of reason, that is to say of the intellect reasoning from its own experiences and thus elaborating scientific knowledge; it is also capable of binding itself by its own laws. If we were to go no further than this level, we might call it pure rationality: and this is probably the level most characteristic of twentieth-century man with his tendency to shut himself up inside a scientific, technical culture. But, deeper still, there is another level, that of the spirit, that dimension of the intellect operating beyond reason and capable of reaching intuitively to the heart of things and to spiritual truths. This level borders on that mysterious centre within us, where the real 'me' dwells, the awareness of our own personality and of our freedom. Down in these depths, which scientific investigation cannot probe, is where the grace of Christ is mysteriously at work. Here, at this inner level of man is where grace is transforming us, and where our will should conquer its freedom. Instead of that, our will usually oscillates between the different levels, having abdicated its proper functions, and allowing its decisions to be made by the emotions or even by the senses, or letting itself be led by the imagination, or seduced into the service of pure rationality. We must learn to anchor our will at the level of the spirit, where Christ reigns, where grace acts and where the Holy Spirit instructs us. If we cannot find the way into this still centre of ourselves, we cannot hear what the Holy Spirit is whispering to us there. At other levels of ourselves, we may think that we can hear him but usually the assertions of our reason or the promptings of our senses or emotions speak much louder. Yes, man is very complex, taken all in all.

The dangerous thing about pure rationality is the way it analyses this complexity—dismantling those mechanisms within reach to find out how they work. And here is a new form of servitude looming up, as we find ourselves being imprisoned by rational psychology.

The same risk applies on the scale of the community. Its soul should be supra-rational love, but instead we may be tempted to stay at the level of what can be achieved by group activity or by purely psychological methods. Admittedly, everything in man is potentially good and true, and his senses can serve to express the most exalted spiritual feelings, conveyed through poetry, music and painting. At the deepest emotional level, he is capable of the noblest heroism. But then, the spirit is ordering all. Scientific discovery, too, particularly advances in psychology, given their due proportion and placed at the service of the spirit, have their value. Everything that is true, everything that is true in its own degree—for there is such a thing as emotional truth, such as rational truth—can be absorbed by the spirit for the development of man and for the way he should live his life.

You must try to make yourself at home in this centre of yourself where God is to be found, so that you can always be listening for the Holy Spirit, and be able to rule your actions by the law of the Gospel. Otherwise you will never conquer your freedom. You will go on being the victim of every kind of slavery. The spirit alone is not a slave; all other levels of human nature are always at risk. The concept of 'interior' life has been pretty strongly disparaged in recent days, people regarding it as a form of individualistic self-indulgence, if not of unhealthy introversion. Interior life can indeed be a refuge from reality. But when genuine, it can be the life of the spirit. True enough, not all interior life is life of the spirit. But in the sense we are using, every one, every Christian, should have a life of the spirit, call it interior life or spiritual life as you please. This spiritual life at its most intense, takes place at a level which is almost impossible to explain. We can easily convey a mathematical problem on the rational level; we can communicate by language on the poetic level, and the same goes for art and music. But when it comes to the divine level, then we find it hard to communicate, except by radiating a love that has its origin in Christ. There is no mistaking the radiance of a genuine spiritual life. The people who went to see the poor Curé d'Ars, who had nothing humanly attractive about him—merely a poor priest with rather limited ideas and a completely conventional theology—recognised him as a man dwelt in by God.

If we learn to strengthen this inner zone, this living in obedience to the Spirit, and to make it the dominant part of us, then the Holy Spirit will be able to quicken our lives, and we shall be able to build a relationship with the Lord in prayer. Sometimes known as theological, since it leads us into the mysterious life of the Three Persons and brings us into habitual communion with the Spirit of Jesus, this is the life that sets us free; through it we rise above habit and the blandishments of transitory things, to that true freedom of the children of God, the strengthener and spiritualiser of our will. Then we can set our heart on what lies beyond the vivid promptings of our imagination, and the uncontrolled impulses of our emotions, and really understand what St Paul means when he speaks of the new man who must be built in us, as opposed to the old man crucified with Christ.

How can we contribute to the building of St Paul's new inner man within us? In as much as we are shaped and enslaved by habits, these must be neutralised by contrary habits freely acquired. St Paul also speaks of the 'unspiritual' man who 'does not accept anything of the Spirit of God', in contrast to the spiritual man who 'on the other hand is able to judge the value of everything, and whose own value is not to be judged by other men'. A religious must not remain an 'unspiritual' man; the climate of religious life, the environment of a community of dedicated brothers, should encourage the spiritual man to develop. The 'unspiritual' man lives at the outer levels of his being, led by his emotions, his senses, his feelings, none of them controlled by the spirit. Hence the need for spiritual discipline, by which we learn to lay decisions and renunciations on ourselves and thus allow the spirit to rule in us and so transform the unspiritual into the spiritual man. This transformation, allowing Christ to reign over our faculties, thus making us truly his, does not take place without self-discipline willingly imposed. How can people fail to understand this today, when technical progress and practice alike require concomitant disciplines in every sphere of life. You can hardly do anything without submitting to some form of discipline. Before take-off, a pilot has to conduct a rigorously disciplined inspection of his aircraft, he has to check everything against a list; he cannot omit a single item without endangering flight-security. We do not always realise the extent of those disciplines accepted by man as he progressively conquers matter by means of increasingly complex machines. The more complex the machine, the less man is its master, indeed he cannot help but become its servant. Computers need men to serve them. And the latter then have no choice but to submit to the machine's own gamut of requirements. Such disciplines, believe me, can be very, very rigorous. They demand great will-power, great concentration, great self-control. So do those of athletes.

But when we come to spiritual disciplines, people seem to have forgotten how important and exacting these are too. The world in which we live, and the world's laws which we have learnt to obey, can easily mislead us here, since the disciplines required by science, though rational and intellectual, are not those suited to spiritual life. Spiritual life has its own special requirements: silence, renunciation, meditation, inner peace. These spiritual disciplines alone can make us pliant in the hands of Christ, make us able to live the fullness of love, make us able to receive the effects of his grace in us. Good intentions and goodwill are not enough. As you know, these spiritual disciplines, by their very nature, cannot be understood by the sensual man, enslaved by his senses, by his emotions or by the lust for pleasure. But they may be equally unintelligible to the purely rational man as well. The purely rational man, imprisoned at the rational level and finding it very hard to go beyond, is largely insensitive to the contemplative dimension and the higher religious values. He, more than anyone, would need to learn how to look at the works of God with the eyes of a child. The rational approach is probably today's greatest single danger to the values of religious life. Even sensuality is made a worse obstacle as a result. Take sexual permissiveness, for instance, which today's rational man takes for granted: what a monstrous perversion! The more you have to do with the worlds of research, technology, science, politics, the more you will realise that almost everywhere the very idea of spiritual and religious discipline is regarded as out of date. We might as well admit this frankly now, rather than make the discovery later. Once again I say, you must be absolutely aware of the demands inseparable from the way that you have chosen to follow.

You may perhaps begin to wonder if there is not some way in which religious life could be adapted to make it intelligible to the modern world. That depends, of course on what you mean by adaptation. I am not talking now about outward forms, since these are relative and subject to change, but to the fundamentals of the Christ-like life and the fundamental disciplines that go with it: as for instance, sacrifice and the cross, the

demands of chastity, poverty and obedience, those values that
we cannot replace by others without altering the Gospel and
the teachings of Christ. We cannot turn our back on the fact
that our dedication binds us to a living, yet crucified, Christ. If
you ask a scientist to adapt himself to a non-scientific environment, he will probably tell you that he cannot turn his back on
what is the most important thing in his life. No more can a
Christian turn his back on his baptismal nature, nor a religious
on his dedicated state, for the sake of adapting himself to an
environment which in any case is changeable and relative. The
history of the evolution of life, as also the struggle man has to
adapt to his present environment, alike show us how man must
stay true to himself and cannot survive unless he subordinates
the environment to his own needs. It is not the environment
that changes man—nor indeed the animal—except perhaps as
to very minor functions, or by accidental mutation. Why then
should the man created in the image of Christ, why should the
religious whose conduct is dedicated by the law of the Gospel
and who has committed himself to a way of life completely
identified with the life of Christ: why should he undergo a
mutation and stop being himself for the sake of adapting to the
environment? That would be going against the law of life. No,
no, it is up to him to influence the environment. Why should the
Christ-like man adapt himself at the risk of destroying himself,
by attenuating the demands of his ideal, which would come to
the same thing as attenuating the demands of Christ himself?
To consent to do this would be grievous, and would in fact
mean destroying the spiritual man. This is the heart of the
problem, and when we look round at all the confusion, muddle-
headedness, loss of confidence and reduction of the demands
made by dedication to God, all threatening the religious life
today, we may be tempted to say that there is no solution. The
life of the spirit, led by faith, has its own laws too: if its basic
vitality is sapped, we fall back into slavery again, becoming
enslaved to the environment, instead of controlling it as Christ
controls it by his Cross and Resurrection.

The religious life, like all Christian life, rests on a number of
indestructible realities: once you doubt these, the whole struc-
ture collapses.

These realities exist on three planes. The first is that of the divine. For our religious life to have meaning, Christ must himself be truly alive, he must be the Son of God and we must be able to give him our lives; the invisible world and the Kingdom of God must be real. The second plane is that of the reality of the spirit: the spirit within us must be immortal, and must be the source of a spiritual life. This is what makes us 'spiritual' men, and allows us to lead a genuine inner life appropriate to the spiritual man. Then there is the third plane: that of the tangible, visible world, in which we are physically immersed. We cannot hope to live the life of the spirit without embodying this spirit in tangible, visible forms; hence the religious life cannot help taking a definite form and being regulated by law and custom. For it is a law of human existence that all spiritual truths must take flesh—a law sanctioned by the incarnation of the Word. From this law flows the need for us to make a constant effort to spiritualise matter and the flesh; which necessity has also been sanctioned by Christ as a redemptive law: that all flesh must achieve life through death, Christ himself having died on the Cross to rise again on the third day. These truths illuminate the law of renunciation, on which depends the vitality of a Christian living in the world and the fulfilment of that dedication pledged by a religious.

5

Brotherly Community and Paschal Mystery

THE CHRISTIANISATION OF our entire nature—for such is the purpose of the Incarnation of the Word—must not only take place in our spiritual life as individuals, but must be apparent in our way of life, impressing itself on our surroundings in such a way as to bring a Christian community into being. A Christian —and I cannot over-stress the importance of this in the world today—cannot grow to perfection except in an ecclesial community. Even a man compelled to live alone, derives his life from the distant community supporting him and rooting him in the Church. With regard to ourselves, the marks of our religious life are to be the three multiple realities of which we spoke last time: divine truths, life of the spirit and embodiment of this life in concrete form.

The Fraternity, like any other religious community, should produce an environment in which the ideal is perfectly embodied. This spirit should permeate even the most lowly, ordinary, humdrum things. The environment bears us and shapes us, while at the same time we create it. The environment is also a sign, expressing a spiritual message within the Church and to the world outside. True, religious communities each have their own way of life and atmosphere, often seeming to permeate the very buildings. The brotherly life used to have its own ceremonies, its own habit, its own chapel. This was important. And to say otherwise would be to deny the basic laws of community life. True, too, this had to change, to be adapted and simplified in all sorts of ways. But should we be wise to abolish every sign, every symbol, the entire religious setting? We are only men after all.

At present, the Church is going through a crisis over how to present herself to the outer world. The Church is looking for a new image. She cannot, however, give up having any image at all, without losing her identity. And, by sharing in the Church's image, religious are also involved in the crisis. We must not allow this to upset us; what we must do is to develop an image corresponding to the essentials of religious life.

Here I might say a passing word about religious dress. I do not want to attach too much importance to the matter. On the other hand, when we think about the nature of the Church and about the needs of people today, particularly about the needs of young people, I do not think that we should dismiss the religious habit too lightly. Whatever people may choose to think, it is neither trivial nor irrelevant. Sociologically speaking, the wearing of uniforms has always been an important method of expression. In every country, in every environment, even the most materialistic, dress conveys meaning. And the abandonment of a certain mode of dress has meaning too. Clothes have had a symbolic significance throughout history. I do not think that this symbolic function will ever disappear, seeing how firmly rooted it is in human mentality. Admittedly, we are now in a time of uncertainty, of trial and error, and experiments have to be made. But we must beware of taking up fixed and final attitudes; we must not lose sight of reality; we must be objective and unprejudiced, equally sensitive to the requirements of the Church and to the true good of other people.

To resume: what should the mode of life be in our Fraternities?

Above all, it should be characterised by the three great renunciations entailed in the threefold profession of chastity, poverty and obedience. I say renunciation quite deliberately, since we must never forget that our profession, however great the love that inspires it, does entail renunciations inseparable from the religious life. I have already explained how these three sacrifices lie at the heart of all Gospel teaching.

God, by the death and resurrection of his son, has given mankind a new and everlasting life. I have said this before, but it is always worth saying again. Today, there is a tendency to overlook the Lord's painful death and to stress his resurrection, apparently in reaction against a medieval and indeed post-medieval spirituality centred on the Lord's passion. The paschal mystery consists, however, of these twin realities of death and life, indissolubly linked. To make an antithesis, or to stress one at the expense of the other, is to err. Besides, we must be realistic: we cannot get away from the fact that we are all on the way to dying, nor that as long as we are living on earth, we are going through our testing-time. This is when death can work in us. If I am wholeheartedly faithful to the passion of Jesus and to what his death should work in me by mortifying the evil and the tendencies to evil, I am assured in my hope of rising again with my Saviour. If, on the other hand, a false view of the Resurrection encourages me to disregard as out of date all sense of mortification, all sense of the Cross and of the need to enter into the death of Jesus, then I cannot be ready when the time comes to rise again with Christ: for no one can rise again unless he has first passed through death. Naturally, I must remember that, if I can conquer evil, I do it by virtue of the life that Christ has won for me by his own victory over evil and death. If we neglect the mystery of the dolorous death of the Saviour, we run the risk of allowing precious aspects of the Redemption to run to waste, and of being less prepared, even now, to live by the grace of the Resurrection—a grace of love, of opening and of transfiguring our lives. But the way into this mystery is not easy. By choosing the religious life, you have chosen the rugged road of the Gospel, you have chosen to enter by the narrow gate. And hence the road of renunciation awaits you: one, though, that leads to life. And you have chosen it because you hunger for the fullness of life, for a life of love; you want everything that life can give, everything that Christ can offer you and give to men, everything that Christ can ask of you in building his Kingdom with him. This is why you must now prepare to give yourself, holding nothing back.

Speaking to those who wish to serve Christ, St Paul invites them to strip themselves naked, since people preparing for a struggle should be as unencumbered as possible. The religious life is an unencumbering. We must get rid of everything that cannot be directly used in the service of Christ, of his Church and of mankind, for the building of the Kingdom of God. We are well aware of having to choose between two different conceptions of human life. Today, we have to make our choice all the more deliberately since, if we choose the conception offered by the religious life in obedience to the Lord, our choice is hardly likely to meet the approval of the world at large. The alternatives are: either to accept the constraint inherent in Christ's law, in the conviction that the Gospel is a law that comes to us from God, and that by obeying its demands we grow greater than we were, become more fully men, and may rightly be called sons of God and may truly become so in the full flowering of the resurrection; or to make up our own law, we now considering ourselves to be as competent to regulate our own behaviour as we are responsible for our own destiny. This latter choice is all the more attractive, since man by virtue of his discoveries about himself has begun to regard the obligations of divine law as no longer binding since in apparent conflict with his self-fulfilment and his right to happiness and success on earth. Armed thus with seemingly water-tight scientific conclusions, we claim the right to decide for ourselves how we should behave.

When we make claims like this, Christ's law seems more demanding than ever, and the keeping of it would in certain cases appear to make earthly happiness impossible. But the real question here is: what do people mean by happiness and success in life? Uncompromising loyalty to the letter of the Gospel law is likely to be very hard in today's cultural environment. The very concept of divine law is being subtly undermined, or interpreted in such a way as to weaken its scope. So you must not be astonished to find the disciplines of religious life, based on the teachings of Christ and on the experience of Christians through the centuries, being systematically attacked in an age of sexual permissivenesss and pure rationality.

We must therefore consider what consequences the application of the Gospel law is going to have in our lives. When I talk of the disciplines of religious life, I mean all those constraints that the religious ought freely to accept, the better to live by the Gospel. We all know what discipline means; what is not so obvious is the relationship between the need for discipline and the fulfilment of the law of love. Let us take an example: the different versions of the *Preface* for Lent. In the old days, there was only one preface, and it spoke of the fruits of mortification as follows: 'by this bodily fasting thou dost curb vice and uplift the mind, bestowing upon us virtue and its rewards . . .'. The new prefaces, of which there are four, take up the same theme but lay more stress on prayer, works of charity and mercy, and on sharing with the hungry. The Church reminds us thus of two complementary aspects of Lenten asceticism. But the present tendency is for Christians to concentrate almost exclusively on the latter to the detriment of the former. We seem to have swung from one extreme to the other—which cannot be good. You see, if we want to pray more and better, and behave more charitably, either this will be so much talk larded with good intentions, or we shall have to make changes in our life. And to make these changes, we shall have to do something to make ourselves capable of praying better and of being more truly and effectively charitable. And this can only be done if we develop the habit of sacrifice and self-discipline and so overcome the permanent obstacle to real change within ourselves. We keep coming back to this—or we keep on talking and talking and getting nowhere. People have a lot to say about love, but the divorce rate keeps rising; a lot to say about peace, but nationalism grows fiercer and so does the class-war; a lot to say about loving the poor, but no class of society is willing to renounce its pursuit of higher purchasing-power for the sake of the third world. We talk about prayer, but do not allow ourselves time to pray. I could go on and on. The sincerest desire to love is not enough: to translate this desire into deeds, you need a will of steel and habitual renunciation and self-control. Yes, we are poor sinners, man is a poor creature and the Lord is infinitely merciful. But we cannot leave it at that; we have to keep struggling. How tragic it is to see them, inspired with such high ideals, yet living in such disorder: young couples divorced at twenty-one, deserting their children: others taking to drugs and total promiscuity: yet full of good will and idealism, champions of gentleness, peace and universal love. But their wills are in fact not free. They seek an instantly realisable ideal. Is this what Christ expects of men whom he has made his brothers? Is this how they should behave? But our worst disorders only go to show more clearly how man craves for the absolute, and how his good will and sincere desire to love cannot produce its fruit because he is no longer able to accept love's real demands. On the plane of the spirit, his will has no strength, enslaved as it is to habits, senses and more than ever to the environment in which he lives.

The religious, however, faced with the same situation, chooses the way of constraint, obliging him to change, to discipline himself, so as to become capable of the greatest love of all. And this is why, now more than ever, the religious way of life must be a leaven. We are not just going to talk about love and prayer; we are going to take the road of love and prayer. We can and must learn to pray, and learn to love. Our apprenticeship is a training, a struggle, a conquering of spiritual freedom; we have to tear out and master the roots of evil and all habits that oppose this freedom. This is what self-discipline is for; asceticism is another word for it, though not much in use now and liable to cause alarm. When all is said and done, however, we cannot do without what the word denotes.

Discipline, asceticism, should rule the whole man, every part of him. Discipline in bearing, in eating, in sleeping: these are all important. And this is usually where we should begin, since many disorders arise, partly at least, from lack of discipline over food, in moments of relaxation and when we are asleep. Discipline must be practised on every one of the planes that we have already discussed. Control of the imagination and memory are particularly important, since we live in cities where the cultural environment is both sexually permissive and materialistic. Otherwise, we strive in a vacuum, to no purpose. As the apostle Paul says: 'I fight, not beating the air. I treat my body hard and make it obey me, for, having been an announcer myself, I should not want to be disqualified.' He does not blench to use such expressions as 'treat *my body* hard' and 'make it obey me'—which fill us with horror today! The discipline is certainly harsh. And he does not merely mean the body as such, but the entire 'unspiritual' entity of our carnal existence.

To this, you may object that such activities are quite out of date and that modern life itself imposes sufficient disciplines of its own: the constraints of work, of urban transport, of timetables, of the environment, of housing and worst of all, of an all-pervading insecurity. Occasions for suffering and constraint enough in our lives, you might think! Of course! Only the mistake lies in supposing that these difficulties of contemporary life, the sufferings they cause and the renunciations they impose, are automatically productive in themselves of balance and self-control in us. Usually the very opposite is true! For them to be an occasion for self-discipline, they have to be accepted in a way conducive to inner discipline. We endure all those constraints of the modern world and, God knows, we know plenty of people so hard-tried by them as sometimes to lose their balance and self-control completely. But it is difficult to learn to endure and even accept these assaults from outside in such a way as eventually to transcend them in love. More usually, far from setting us free, they enslave us, sometimes so much that they distort our character.

Nothing, therefore, should deter us from seeking a discipline that we can impose freely on ourselves. This will make it easy for us to accept all the renunciations and sufferings that life can offer, and turn them to a greater good. If you cannot renounce an immediate pleasure because of force of habit or weakness of will, you will not know how to cope with occasions for renunciation offered by modern life.

Basically, we are always faced with the same problem: the spirit, with vigour renewed and transfigured by Christ, has to invest all matter, every aspect of life; only by reigning in man's heart can the spirit master the universe, in such a way that man can conquer it and not be enslaved by it. The spirit invests all things, all external things, by love and for love. The centre of the universe will always be a man's heart. But a man's heart would no longer be so, were it a cauldron of seething passions. Each man, by virtue of his heart, is the centre of the universe. I use the word 'heart' here in its deep, biblical sense: the centre of a man and of all that makes him a living being, the source of good but also of evil, the secret, hidden place where God can reach me, the seat of conscience. This, the heart, centre of my life and of all that I am, is what has got to be transformed, purged and renewed.

The way of pain and struggle which we are obliged to follow, leads us back to the mysterious death that took place in the naked suffering of the Cross, and to the hope of the Resurrection. I use the word 'mysterious' advisedly, since even after centuries of meditation, theologians have still not been able to explain why Jesus had to endure such a painful passion and death. There are depths here, enigmas that defeat even theology. Why such prodigality of suffering and abjection? Why this mysterious sacrifice? Today people tend to play down the sacrificial aspect of the Saviour's death on the Cross, and to see it rather as the death of one poor innocent, hounded and unjustly sentenced by the courts, and incarnating the daily suffering and injustice endured by the world's oppressed millions. And thus we sidestep the mysterious divinisation of man at the price of Christ's agony on the Cross. What is really significant about the passion of Jesus, is that he endured death, humiliation and the abasement of contempt and mockery because of his functions as the Messiah. Being a king, he was hit, wearing a crown of thorns and the derisive purple, while the charge against him, posted on the wood of the Cross, sarcastically proclaimed his royal title: 'This is Jesus, King of the Jews'. Being a prophet, he was beaten, he the Word of God, the very Word made man; they blindfolded him and beat him, saying: 'Play the prophet! Who hit you then?' Being high priest, he was humiliated, offering himself as victim for the most humiliating sacrifice of all, the torment of the Cross. No, the human mind could never explain such a death, nor reduce it to the execution of a victim of human injustice, not to mention his position as Son of God, as High Priest, by his blood opening for us the gates of the Kingdom yet to come: so that his passion henceforth has a fundamental relevance for every one of us in our relationship with God.

Brother Charles lived this mystery of pain and joyful hope very deeply, and so was able to enter into the mystery of the Eucharist as deeply as he did. The Eucharist is our perpetual memorial of the passion of Jesus. For us, participation in the act of eucharistic sacrifice is not enough. Certainly, we need to participate sacramentally in the passion of our Saviour; but we must also make our lives conform to it in every detail at every minute of the day. This is why the Eucharist is always to be found in our Fraternities; hence the importance of the act of silent adoration by which each of us is called to give his life to the Eucharist. Our obedient and loving communion with the will of the Crucified, freely laying down his life for us, should result in a deep transformation of our nature. From the passion of Jesus we should receive the spiritual strength to conquer all evil and to make all suffering fruitful. The strength given by the Lord does not show in startling ways, it is not always even felt since, everything within us being the work of God, we cannot consciously detect it. But Jesus is there, constantly at work. And the Cross is there too, whichever way we go to reach Christ; the Cross is always on the road leading to him, obliging us to rise above ourselves; the Cross constantly purges and finally prepares us for our meeting with the Lord. Whichever way we take, we have to go by the Cross.

The baffling mystery of human suffering and evil can only be rightly understood, can only acquire a meaning, when linked to the passion of Jesus. All our human sorrows have to be trans-figured by this mystery—from within. And then they become a source of strength, of life, and the seed of resurrection. In this world, we should speak of the seed of resurrection, rather than of resurrection. And in this context we see what Brother Charles meant by 'the taste for voluntary sacrifice'. As he saw it, the passion of Jesus was totally free and voluntary; whereas another man might have undergone the same, accepting it freely perhaps, but certainly not willing it. With Christ, how-ever, the suffering was willed, since no one could take his life away from Him. He had to lay it down freely, by a personal act of will.

If therefore we wish to be like Christ and have a part in his passion, we shall probably have to go further than merely accepting the crosses on our way; love will urge us on to take our own willing part in the passion of our Saviour. Jesus endured the passion in his humanity, although he was the Word who had created all things; he identified himself completely with his Father's will, subordinating his own in a supreme act of obedience. That is why there is a special connection between willing sacrifice and the work of Christ. We must learn to accept every occasion for suffering that may arise, now that we understand the meaning of this path; it leads to life. We must never be afraid of suffering; we must banish all fear on this score. A Christian should never be afraid. Brother Charles used to say: 'One of our absolute duties to our Lord is never to be

afraid of anything'. Of course, we may be tempted to be afraid,
just as Jesus was in Gethsemane. Let us lead our lives courageously and refuse to dwell on imaginary dangers to come. If we
concentrate on the present, we shall have a better grasp of what
life demands of us and we shall not be afraid.

Voluntary sacrifice, far from being a morbid taste for suffering, is in fact a sign of energy; it is a realistic, life-giving attitude
and, by setting us free, makes us ready to undertake all things,
to accept all things and, above all, to sympathise with all human suffering. Other people's sufferings frighten us, since we
try instinctively to shield our own peace of mind. We fear the
Cross. Yet the lives of the saints who suffered, some of whom
were mysteriously and closely associated with the passion of
Christ, show the almost infinite efficacity of suffering in union
with the suffering of the Saviour of the world. What man regards instinctively as the most horrible reality of all, takes on
inestimable worth in Christ, by Christ. We cannot understand
this properly; perhaps only saints and contemplatives can.
The world is, as it were, surrounded by the Cross, the yard-
stick of all human values.

Instead of incessantly complaining in religion about what
makes us suffer and what we try to avoid—in the brotherly life,
for instance, or when we have to obey—we ought to remind ourselves that this is what we wanted in the first place. Yes, we
chose it, knowing what it would be like; we were never so deluded as to imagine that religious life would be a softer option
than any other. Admittedly, if we were only to think of religious
life under its concrete, human aspect, and not in its aspect as
dedication to Christ, it might seem petty and restricted, sometimes engrossed in petty, personal and community problems, and
therefore tending to be self-absorbed, when it could and should
ever be witnessing to its own deeper nature as a brotherly,
ecclesial community centred on the Eucharist and on the Lord;
and outgoing through love. The Fraternity, like any Christian
or religious community, begets us in pain, but brings us to birth
for a more abundant life. The Church brings us to both: we
should not complain if the process is occasionally painful: for
there is no child-bearing without pain, and life begins in suffering; such is the universal law. No birth occurs without pain:
we are born to Christ daily. This is what I should like you to

learn in the Fraternity, even and especially when the Fraternity makes you suffer.

The chapel where we are now gathered, is impregnated with the long hours Brother Charles spent here in communion with Christ, his beloved Saviour. Like thousands of other Christians, he used the devotion of the Way of the Cross as his means of participating in the passion of the Lord. The white, wooden plaques, designed by him, mark the stations on the thick earthen pillars. Nowadays people do not set much store by this devotion. And although it is quite in order that our ways of expressing devotion should change with the times, it would be a very serious matter, were we to forget how to show our humble, loving participation in the sufferings of Jesus, which for their part transcend all time. The history of the Church and of Christian spirituality enriches us with an experience that is never ending. How wrong we should be to think that we have reached a kind of break in Christian evolution, meaning that the past no longer has relevance for us. History shows us that the saints have always known how to rise above one-sided reactions. We ourselves are now in danger of letting ourselves be carried away by one such, inducing us to reject *a priori* many values of the past. Most of the great Councils have taken place in times of change and have often been followed by over-reaction: as a result of which quite a long time has been needed before the Council's guidance could be assimilated and the balance between opposing tendencies redressed. I say this with reference to the cult of the passion of the Saviour; it would be equally true of other topics but I do not propose to enlarge on this.

6

The Promise Made in Love

I NOW WANT to consider another aspect of the religious life: its natural tendency to become stable and permanent. This is why it is a 'vowed' or 'consecrated' life, that is to say, one bound by sacred pledges. That religious life should be stable and permanent hardly seems a mark of perfection these days, or desirable or even possible. Indeed the modern world encourages us to prize drive, movement and change; where everything is regarded as evolving, stability must needs appear a fault. Stability looks like the antithesis of movement, hence the negation of progress: whereas change is hailed as indispensable to progress.

It is of course true that all progress does entail change: we have to change in order to improve. But we should remember that change can also be a sign of instability and of decadence rather than of progress. For there to be progress, change has to be always in the same direction. Otherwise there will be no progress and all you will have will be changeability. Not every change is perforce a change for the better.

Stability, when we use the word in connection with religious life, is not the same as inertia: it means stability of direction towards a given aim. We do not settle into an inert life but, fixing our eyes on the goal, resolve never to deviate from that. Hence, as we shall see, religious stability is not an interior state but a way of living which helps us to keep on our right course. If you like, you could compare stability to railway-lines allowing us to travel much faster in a given direction. The rails are

not any old rails: but a line laid by the Lord and maintained
by the Church. Any movement requires that you should know
your goal and stick to it. To generate the power, to start moving, to make progress, there has to be an engine: the motor-
power of love. Now, all love has one goal: the beloved. You
would not think love were perfect, if it looked likely to keep
changing its object. And the changeability so characteristic
of modern life consists precisely in endless changes of object.

Love's need for stability is illustrated in the history of the Old
Covenant. In contrast to the faithfulness, constancy and infinite patience of God, the Chosen People were inconstant and
fickle. This is our own life-story too: every one of us. God un-
sparingly tries to set his people on the right course; he lays
down a permanent way, fixes the lines: that is the Law and the
incessant warnings of the Prophets. And it only needs Moses
to tarry on the mountain top for the people to lose faith in him
and hark back to the past, frustrating the whole venture by
reverting to the gods of Egypt. We too are all too prone to
change our goal. You need only look around you. In any case,
why not change? Since nothing that man is now pursuing can
satisfy him, the search must switch to another direction. The
perpetual need for change comes from a feeling of dissatisfac-
tion: whereas stability in one same direction indicates that the
goal pursued corresponds to our deepest desires, and that our
thirst to attain it grows greater all the while. We, for our part,
shall never be satisfied either, but this is because our stability
is directed towards the infinite and the absolute.

Here we come back to what we have already been saying
about the law of the senses and the law of the spirit. The senses
lead us to desire continual change, since we quickly get bored
and boredom then urges us to something different. The outer
level of our nature is constantly being affected by boredom.
Boredom can insinuate its way into the very heart of love. Love
for another human being as changeable as ourselves, is easily
eroded by boredom. Hence, the mystery of the indissolubility
of marriage, compelling us to look, through the lens of human
love, at that infinite something that every individual has: the
transcendent dimension of his nature, made in the image of
God. Life is short, and whatever is demanded by constancy in
love can at most last for only a few years, until we die. Is that

asking so much? The vicissitudes of love are characteristic of the human condition; at the same time, they reflect a yearning for eternity.

Man finds death baffling. Death is something beyond his power to imagine, he has no way of picturing it. No one can imagine what death is like since, being the end and negation of all physical activity, it cannot be grasped by our physical faculties. Death defeats the imagination. What, however, one can imagine is one's death-agony, the process of dying—but not death itself. None the less, death does exercise a fascination over men, and those who have exhausted every kind of pleasure and grown sick of a life with nothing left to offer them, turn to death as the only stable, fixed and eternal state within their reach. This is a perversion of the true purpose of life by people who have nowhere else to turn.

But we can see that it is quite normal for people to feel a need for security, for a basic security. In this respect, man is ever a child; and a child cannot develop and achieve a proper emotional balance without the security of the home. Insecurity is traumatic for a child. And so it is for an adult. I do not mean the security contrived by selfishness, nor the security of wealth, nor of any other sort of rejection of the risks entailed in any great-hearted enterprise, but the security afforded by a great love, and the basic security of knowing for certain that life has a purpose—without which conviction no one can live. We need a home-port.

And this is the security offered by faith, Church and religious life. And that is why religious life contains one element that many people find alarming: I mean, the stability of a life directed towards a single goal, none other than Christ. Stability is now to be seen as a way of self-transformation, a way pointed out to us by Christ. If the religious life is undertaken for love—and it cannot be undertaken without it, for then there would be no vocation—for love of Christ, a love beyond mere words and transcending all emotions, how could this be other than forever?

What is stable in the religious life is not our interior state but the content of our religious commitment, which is a way, a way of life. For the rest, as far as giving ourselves to loving God and our brothers is concerned, we shall each go as far along this path as we can. I do not think that we should make a vow of total love; there would be no point in it, since we are already bound to this by the Lord. But we can freely choose to belong to a community, choose the way of dedicated celibacy, the way of deprivation and total sharing in brotherly life, and choose to leave responsibility for our lives to Christ, to put it bluntly, by obedience, by depriving ourselves of the possibility of choosing another goal. By doing this, we commit ourselves to a way of life, to a state of life (although the term is hardly understood these days). In olden days, people were always talking about states of life; they talked of the married state; when you chose a career, you spoke of choosing a 'state of life'. People knew that they were committing themselves to something stable and permanent. Note, people still do it, but the future is so uncertain and things change so fast that young people committing themselves to a profession today, feel insecure in doing so; they feel, quite rightly, that after ten or twenty years their professional qualifications will be out of date and that periodic refresher-courses are not going to prevent their being replaced by younger men. Such is the world today: unstable, uncertain with endless change foreseen. In contrast to this, the religious life has stability. The religious life forces us to discover, deep down within us, that point where our life is already locked into eternity.

But why take vows? Couldn't we embrace an evangelical way of life without binding ourselves to do so? Certainly, we could. And the fact that we are now going to consider the peculiarly religious significance of vows taken before God, does not in the least imply that the religious life is the only way of following the evangelical path. Any Christian is at liberty to promise celibacy for the Lord's sake, to practise poverty either on his own or by joining a group and living in a brotherly community: all this is perfectly possible and some people do indeed do this and do it well. The religious life is not simply the evangelical path: there is another factor, to which we are called and which is precisely expressed by promises.

This making of promises is not exactly popular today. People are rather suspicious about it. It strikes them as of no value, as merely legalistic. What is the point of making promises? Why not just live as the Gospel tells us? There is no need to bind ourselves by a vow. It adds nothing to the life as it is led. Indeed, you might say that the very fact of promising and binding ourselves tends to institutionalise religious life, which is the last thing we want to do. And further, this promising is going to lose us the merit of 'spontaneity' or 'creativity'—to use the current terms. Mustn't we be absolutely free of all bonds to be spontaneous, love being spontaneous? Some people have this attitude so deeply engrained that they are really incapable of making promises. I was recently told of an unmarried couple who had been living faithfully together for years and years in perfect harmony. Someone advised them to consecrate this faithfulness in the marriage bond. Which they did. No sooner were they married than the problems began, and they were divorced in a matter of months. The fact of having ratified their union by a formal promise had demoralised them completely.

This is of course an exceptional case, but indicative all the same of the sort of difficulties that some people may have. Is faithfulness without promise preferable to promise without faithfulness? I am not talking about marriage now. As regards the evangelical life, why not be satisfied with a life genuinely given in love? Isn't love the only true bond? Then why make promises? Would it be because I need a guarantee against my own instability? Why, yes! But isn't that a very second-rate solution; doesn't it show a lack of trust in the grace of the Lord? Wouldn't it be better to trust in God, day after day, relying on his grace? There is a grain of truth in all these objections. And there are several delusions too. And the true value of the promise is to be found on a quite different plane.

These attitudes are over-idealistic; we must take a more realistic view. As regards the psychological obstacles, these need to be seen in perspective, valid as they well may be. But if we examine the question on psychological premises alone, we shall get stuck at the level of the unspiritual man, without rising to that of the spiritual, of the Christ-like, man. If we are only prepared to examine problems in psychological terms, this is surely a proof that we have lost our awareness of other values. We need perhaps to re-educate ourselves to rise above such difficulties, rather than allow ourselves to be imprisoned by the 'unspiritual man'.

We should take our stance at the level of what ought to be a great love affair, a spiritual love affair: whether our love for God and his Christ, or our love for men, a love ceaselessly renewed by the power of God's own love, made new in Christ and coming to us in him. Love desires to give all. Then let love express itself according to its own nature. Do not hold back, do not be held back by reasons over-rational. Love has laws that are not rational. You stifle love if you keep raising objections. Love wants to give all, and giving all means giving your life, your whole life. What then is our whole life?—our past life? My life is what it has been, good or bad: I cannot change that now. But it is within my power to repent, and then I can only love my merciful Saviour the more. My life to come? Can I dispose of my future? I do not own that yet; how can I give it away? How fertile in illusions our future is! With our imagination making us live in the future and our memory making us live in the past, we forget the passing of time and the mysterious fullness of the present. Yet life is only measured to us second by second. We never own it all. And so we cannot give it all, except by means of a free and willing promise. This is the only way in which we can overcome the infinitely narrow limitations of the present. The only way in which love can give all at once, is by making a promise. This strengthens our personality, raising us above our instant life to grasp the whole entire. By promising, we achieve control of time. Yes, this is very true. Perhaps I shall die tomorrow, having given only one day to the Lord, but if, in the great love that fills my heart, and with my whole will, I have pledged myself to God until death, I shall truly have given my whole life—in intention—and if I have been sincere, I have given true proof of my love.

People may say what they please: the promise is also a guarantee of faithfulness. For our promise—unless we are deluded—is concerned with very concrete matters of daily life: we pronounce it in a community and it binds us to our brothers. This is certainly not to be discounted. Our promise also binds us to a rule. Ask yourself in all honesty what would have happened to you in such-and-such circumstances, if you had had neither community, nor rule, nor superior? Be humble and realistic enough to admit it! On the pretext of a perfection that takes no account of human frailty, we put ourselves in the position of being unable to do what is right. Why, for instance, used the

Church to oblige her priests to recite the breviary? I use the past tense, since the Church expresses her will more subtly today. Because the Church wished her priests to pray in her name. Yet prayer only has value if it is an act of love, freely performed. Why not merely recommend priests to pray faithfully for the Church? Let's face it: even priests with a sense of prayer and of the mission entrusted to them by the Church, found this duty easier to fulfil because of this feeling of obligation. You could say as much of the obligations fundamental to any religious rule.

Isn't there a kind of pride in this denying of value to an obligation or to a religious rule? Or at least a misunderstanding of the humble demands of human nature? It is true; let us admit it: a promise is a guarantee. How could you dare to forget how weak your will is, and claim to be able to follow the arduous road of the Gospel, alone, unaided either by a rule or by the support of your brothers? It cannot be done. Yes, there are a few exceptional vocations: calls to the solitary life, or to solitary life in the world. But these could not be pursued without obligations either.

The guarantee of faithfulness is the effect of our promise; it is not our motive for making it. We promise out of love, because this is a promise made to God. And thus, we rise above the fleeting minute to experience even now a foretaste of eternity. This sort of promise only makes sense because we are destined for eternity. A life-long promise would lose its meaning if all ended with death. People hesitate today to lead their lives on the basis of a hereafter. They do not give much thought to the fact that life is eternal, or at least do not have lively enough convictions about it to influence their actual behaviour. So I can quite understand why they cannot grasp the scope or the true reason for making a promise binding forever.

7

Dedicated to Christ and His Church

WE HAVE SEEN that the religious vocation requires us to translate our love for God into promises, and that these will affect every detail of our lives. Our commitment takes the form of a pledge made to God and we call this a vow. There are certain objections that can be raised against vows. Some people consider the devotion to be out of date and unsuited to modern Christian life. So what is a vow? A promise made to God, nothing more, but again nothing less. Its great value and peculiar character reside in the fact that the promise is made to God himself. For a creature to venture to respond to his Creator by making him a promise, is a very serious matter, since a promise of this sort, however interior, however private, binds very strictly, very weightily. We cannot invoke the name of God lightly—unless, that is, we have no idea what we are doing. So, I say, the importance and value of the vow depend on the intentions of the person uttering it.

I shall not go over the content of the vows again, since we have already discussed this. The vows are the building-blocks of religious life. What we are promising is to live in accordance with the precepts of the Gospel. But some promises made to God entail a special dedication.

What do we mean when we talk of 'dedicating ourselves' or of 'being dedicated'? They do not mean the same thing. Are we the ones who are doing the dedicating, or is God the one who is dedicating us? And why does the vow dedicate the person who pronounces it? These are questions for which we must find answers.

First of all, let's take the word in its more ordinary sense, as for instance when we say that someone is dedicating his life to scholarship, or to caring for the sick—which might or might not be a full-time activity. We mean by this that the activity (whatever it is) is his ruling pre-occupation and that everything he does—his thoughts and deeds—are concentrated on it. Often, of course, the expression 'dedicate oneself to something' is used in a loosely metaphorical way. But when we say that someone has dedicated his life so utterly to scientific research that he has decided to stay free for it by not getting married, his dedication ceases to be metaphorical. For such a seeker, the acquisition of knowledge has become a governing pre-occupation, and to achieve it he has subordinated all his powers and indeed his whole way of life. You have a life entirely built round a great ideal; and when this ideal happens to be the exclusive service of God himself, dedication takes on its fullest, religious sense. The word takes on its most rigorous sense, and we cannot use it any other way where God is concerned. Because I want to dedicate my life to God, I work with all my might exclusively to establish his kingdom on earth, and I take the path of chastity by practising celibacy—which in turn becomes dedicated too. I take this path for God's sake and because it leads to him, and I have to practise it to prepare myself properly for meeting God after this life. I take it in poverty, that is to say, by renouncing all wealth, in every sense of the word. Including the exercising of power, or the achieving of any work that will be truly mine—since my life is exclusively and entirely given to, 'dedicated' to, the things of God.

This does not mean, that I shall not use human resources, but that in everything my intention will be guided by the intentions of the Lord himself and by the desire to establish his Kingdom. Because of this, I freely renounce control over my own activities, since they too are dedicated. I also renounce doing what I myself want to do, since, if I am logical about my commitment, I can now only wish and desire one thing: to serve God by doing his will, and to serve his Church. Henceforth I am at the Church's disposal; she will tell me what I am to do. This is how the vows of chastity, poverty and obedience consecrate my life and my person to the service of God and his Church. The vows may only seem to have bearing on certain aspects of my life, but in fact they involve the gift and sacrifice of the whole of me.

Alas, the ideal of dedication can degenerate; it starts losing its strength and exclusive character, once we forget that it binds us to a person, to a divine person. I am actually dedicated to God, to Jesus Christ; and, because I belong to him, I am automatically dedicated to doing what he wants of me. But since we are in the world, we shall always be strongly tempted to forget that we are dedicated to the invisible person of Jesus Christ, and be inclined to regard our dedication merely in terms of apostolic activity—which is human activity none the less. We then begin to pervert our dedication from its proper end: which is the gift of ourselves to the divine power of the Son of God.

Dedicated to the works of the Kingdom, we can also be tempted into dedicating ourselves to activities only marginally concerned with our proper apostolate. And these can become as engrossing as any other job. Yes, it can happen; we can see men and women in religion, whose dedication to the Lord has degenerated into a round of activities or a way of life for which they would be hard put to remember either the original meaning or ultimate purpose.

Religious dedication implies that all our doings should be subject to the Lord. We have seen how this happens in the common brotherly life when each member lives it as a gift of himself to the person of Jesus Christ. Our way of life must lead us to be more and more like Him whom we have lovingly chosen to follow. And for this we have the magnificent example of Brother Charles of Jesus—since everything that happened in his life happened as a result of his absolute and basic need to be like the One he loved. Besides, religious dedication only makes sense when it expresses a very great love and when the practice of the vows makes it easier for us to love more intensely still.

There is more to dedication however than this. You were not the ones to take the initiative and decide of your own accord to take your life and give it to God, for it to be radically reshaped by the evangelical demands of serving him. God first called you. So it is for God to approve and accept this dedication of your

life. And since God is God, he will dedicate you, he will lay his
hand on you. And once God has laid his hand on you, you must
be faithful. I cannot do better than refer you again to accounts
of vocations related in the Bible.

But, where we are concerned, perhaps you will object—
unlike in the Bible stories—God never speaks. So how can we be
sure that God accepts our dedication? How do we know that
God has dedicated us, that he has really said: 'Henceforth I
have laid my hand on you and accepted the gift of your life to
use it as I please.' Under the Old Covenant, God used to appear to those whom he was to charge with a prophetic mission.
Under the New, he does not do this any more, having entrusted
all things to his Son, who has himself entrusted this power to his
Church. Today there is a widespread tendency to minimise
this function of the Church. Yet Jesus has done this: he cannot
be present to us and we cannot communicate with him, except
through his Church. We can never say this too often: outside
the Church, we are on our own, lonely seekers of the way. Yes,
to be sure, the Lord's grace is at work everywhere, but inside
the Church we are actually able to hear his voice, to ask him
questions, to offer ourselves to him and receive an answer given
in his Name. This is how Jesus is ever present for us within the
Church. Hence the fundamental difference between a promise
made to God in the heart, privately, and a promise made to God
publicly, in the Church: for the Church receives our promise
and dedicates us in Christ's name, and in dedicating us, has the
right to tell us what she expects of us by virtue of this dedication. Henceforth we are at her service, not at ours; God has laid
his hand on us, and God's hand is the hand of the Church.

We are therefore dedicated in Christ's name. But here another question springs to mind: how does religious dedication
differ in nature from baptismal dedication and the sacrament
of marriage. For in St Paul we find some very emphatic words
about the way the sacrament of marriage gives rise to a mysterious union which the Apostle has no qualms in comparing
to the union between Christ and his Church. It is as though the
basic social unit of the Christian home reproduces in little the
ecclesial character of the great society, the Church. Religious
dedication also gives rise to a mysterious union: a covenant between the dedicated soul and Jesus. And if we wish to compare

these two covenants, we shall say that the marriage covenant, sacramentally speaking, is linked to the Divine Covenant not so much directly but through the creation of a Christian home, something therefore temporal and transitory. A husband who loves his wife, and a wife who loves her husband, both knowing themselves to be joined together in God's name for the rest of their lives, form a very exalted union, reflecting God's covenant with his people. But this relationship with the Covenant is realised in a non-immediate way, marriage being a temporal institution. Religious profession on the other hand anticipates the eternal Kingdom, it is already part of the Kingdom to come. This is something we must never forget if we want to understand the value of religious dedication. You see, the more aware we are of the value of the world, the better we understand the value of marriage; and the more aware we are of the things of eternity, the better we understand the value of religious dedication. Now you can see why by today's lights, marriage seems more important than religious profession: men being prisoners of the temporal even when, as Christians, they dedicate themselves very selflessly to temporal activities.

If you look again at what the last Council had to say about the religious life, you will see it defined as a state of closest proximity to Christ: the religious follows Christ very closely; he is bound to Christ's Church and dedicated to her service.

Out of respect for the value of every calling within the Church, people are reluctant to compare the varying merits of marriage, priesthood, religious life and so forth. And certainly the finest and best vocation for anyone is the one to which he himself is called. For myself, however, I know that when Jesus called me and I answered him, I did this because I was determined to follow him as closely as I could. Were there no difference between being a married man and being a religious, why choose to be a religious? The reason is that, just as the sacrament of marriage is a true fulfilment of baptism and the obligations of Christian life dependent on it at one level, so religious profession, whatever be its form, fulfils baptismal dedication even more completely by supplementing it. I say by supplementing it, since baptismal dedication is not a static but a dynamic state; it is conferred on us as the seed of a Christian life which still has to be lived; and religious profession comes at the later stage of adult response to the obligations proceeding from baptism, as a result of which we live for God. Once you have been baptised, the way you fulfil your baptismal commitment is by growing in the mystery of Christ; religious profession has no other object than to assure this growth in Christ in a more constant and radical way. A Christian should have no difficulty in understanding this. And in any case there is no problem here for anyone who lives close to God or has received a call to the religious life.

Nevertheless, there are varying degrees and forms of dedication to the evangelical way. And when the Church tells us that she attaches particular importance to religious profession and to the dedication that goes with it, she also acknowledges that there are other types of dedication—as for instance that of groups living the common life and taking other sorts of vows, or that of secular institutes. But, in the judgment of the Church, these other types of dedication are less absolute, they are different, they are less completely imprinted with the character of the Kingdom of God to come, since they do not entail the same consequences as religious profession where temporal activities are concerned.

The religious life is not a middle way. A religious intends to dedicate himself body and soul; God dedicates him; the Church dedicates him; and the dedication binds him to a community governed by a rule of life. This latter aspect of profession is often overlooked. Religious dedication is not a private event; you are dedicated in and for a community. If you leave it, you lose your dedication, since you can only fulfil this properly in union with your brothers and your superiors. Thus, the community too has a share in your dedication: the community has to accept you and assume responsibility—with you—for your promises. This is a very important aspect of brotherly love, closely linked to the mystery of the Church.

I am not going to repeat what I have already said about the importance of the community and of the sharing entailed by it. But I ought to remind you that, by virtue of your profession, you should all aim at being only of one heart and one soul. You will not always succeed, but the reality is always there, urging you to live this way.

The Church has authenticated the soul of our community by

approving our rule. Profession is bound to this rule; no one can make a religious profession except in accordance with a Rule. Why?—because words in themselves are not enough; we do not give ourselves to God in some vague or general way. Would it be enough to dedicate ourselves to God like this: I promise to obey the Gospel? All Christians are bound by the Gospel and ought to obey it. You have chosen to follow a special path, and any dedication—if not an empty form—ought to be related to the special concrete conditions pertaining to the way chosen. Everyone has his own life to lead; everyone's life is different. We cannot therefore live the particular in a general way, or according to some theory or other. Our life takes one particular form. That is why the religious Rule is so important and has to be constantly renewed, the better to fit its purpose. It ought to be the true expression of the chosen ideal, and the Church reserves the right to approve this. The Church could not agree to accept the dedication of someone not willing to dedicate himself to a rule approved by her, since she herself has the responsibility of authenticating our path in the Lord's name.

The rule points the lines along which we are to fulfil our dedication, by fixing its main concrete requirements. It also defines the matter in which we pledge ourselves to serve the Church. For when you become a servant, you do not reckon to do what you want, but what your Master wants. A religious is only a servant of the Church, and this he has to be completely. Serving the Church is the basic idea behind the vow of obedience. You no longer have the right to choose how you will serve. This attitude of being ready to serve in any way allowed the Virgin Mary to sum up her whole vocation and to do all that was demanded of her, by thinking of herself as only, but absolutely, 'the handmaid of the Lord'. Her attitude sums up our vocation too; we have no more to add. A religious knows that, having made his profession, he has nothing further to say about how his life should be used. His personal, private life has been taken away from him; in exchange, he has been given the status of a servant, a life in the service of the Lord and of his brothers. The promise to serve can be given in a moment, but it takes a whole lifetime to work it out; and that will not be done without a sharp struggle. It would be silly to think that we were following the Lord closely, if we were eagerly to take every side road rather than pass by Calvary. The way of obedient service is a narrow road, but it leads to Life.

I conclude with a few words on a fairly common contemporary attitude: that of criticising the laws and rules of the Church as artificial and legalistic. This is a reaction against very real abuses. But without going into this too deeply, I should just like to say that people cannot live together without a minimum of law to guarantee them the freedom and respect due to them as individuals. Every community, every society, has to have a body of laws, or you would have anarchy. No society can survive in a state of anarchy, least of all a religious community.

Now, it is true that this giving of ourself to the Lord takes place in the recesses of the heart. Neither Church nor superiors can ever penetrate into the sanctuary of conscience, where you are alone with the voice of God. As far as your love for God or your love for your brothers is concerned, you and you alone can give it or withhold it. You alone can decide whether to make it grow, or play safe and do little. What the Church has to offer you is a rule, a community, an environment, a way. What she holds out to you is a way of living which you promise the Lord to observe. But this way of living impinges on the depths of the heart, like the state of celibacy for instance and above all the state of dependence on the rule and on your superiors. This is why obedience is hard.

Before leaving the subject of the community and religious dedication, I must remind you that seeds will not germinate unless the soil is right. The Lord himself emphasised this in one of his most striking parables, by going to the pains of explaining it to his apostles. I mean the Parable of the Sower. The seed has all the potentialities of growth, flowers and fruit; it contains all this; all the energy is there; but it cannot germinate if the soil is not right. Now, we are the soil, and the function of the religious life is to help prepare the soil; the religious life provides the means for doing this. The seed that falls by the wayside is quickly carried off by the birds: it has not even been recognised for what it is. The Evil One comes 'and carries off what was sown in that man's heart'. Then there is the stony ground, where there is very little soil and where the seed cannot strike root, and so dries out: there is no depth. We have to plough our hearts deep. Once you are only left with mediocre aspirations, once you retreat into yourself, once you shut yourself up in a more or less self-centred attitude to life, you have no depth of soil. But ploughing deep is not enough, for some fields are overgrown with brambles and other weeds, which the Lord tells us are the worries of this world and the lure of riches. If your vow of poverty does not make you willing to tear these brambles and other weeds out of your heart where they bid fair to choke the Lord's seed, this is a sign that you are not poor as the Lord would have you poor. Poverty that does not clear the heart's ground for the Word of God to come to better fruiting, is a mere material poverty: and not enough. Beware of any poverty as a delusion, if it does not first and foremost entail the harsh reality of renouncing all sorts of things that we can do without but which we love so dearly. Let your own poverty reflect that evangelical poverty of which Christ himself is our examplar.

8

Silence and Prayer

———————

LAST TIME WE mentioned the Parable of the Sower and the
Seed; this leads us on to the thought that religious life ought to
provide an environment favourable to the growth of another
sort of seed: the seed of prayer. In religious life, this ought to
develop easily and bear fruit. And by religious life, I do not only
mean your personal dedicated life, but also the environment
constituted by the Fraternity, the brotherly community; as
also by the way we sincerely and convincedly observe the basic
rules making the Fraternity what it is and giving it its particular
spiritual character. Yes, materially, humanly and psychologic-
ally speaking, the Fraternity should generate an environment favourable to the germination and development of
prayer.

I am now talking of prayer generally, without distinguishing
between the various forms of prayer: liturgical prayer, Eucharistic adoration, intercessory prayer. No, I mean prayer as including all these and going further still. I mean the prayer that
wells up in the depths of the heart, like a great river fed by its
several tributaries but as to its main-stream essentially ever the
same. Whether prayer be in its early stages or more advanced,
whether it be short or long, whether more or less habitual, the
gift, always essentially the same, comes to us from the Lord,
who carries us away by his Spirit.

Christian prayer is the germinating of the Word of God. It is
the Word of God bearing fruit in an intellect enlightened by
faith, and in the heart, to lead us by the obscure light of in-

creasing love ever deeper into the mystery of God. Within which mystery, every human being is destined to come to fulfilment in heart's union with the Eternal. Prayer is something within us leading us towards fullness of life.

How are we to talk about prayer? People are always asking whether prayer can be learnt, like learning an art such as drawing, painting or music. People with experience of prayer do not need to be taught what it is, and those who have not yet had the experience, can only half grasp—and then only in theory— what they are told about it. As for those who have given up prayer and have lost a taste for it even though still yearning for it, they need only set to praying again to rediscover how sweet it is. We can certainly talk about prayer, and so we should. The contemplatives have told us all its secrets. But prayer is always beyond the power of words to describe, since it is not circumscribed by reason. Prayer, being contact with divine life at its source, contains an element not susceptible of definition, even though this divine life reaches us through the humanity of Christ. This life, adapted to our own nature through Christ, can penetrate and raise us to loving intuition of the very reality of God and of all his divine activities. All genuine prayer is, or is potentially, contemplative, and the work of the Spirit of Jesus within us. The Apostle Paul tells us that 'God has sent the Spirit of his Son into our hearts: the Spirit that cries, Abba Father!' The ability to pray to God as to a father is the distinguishing characteristic of Christian prayer and the expression of our adoption by him. Prayer is the awareness and development of the Christian's essential cry: 'Abba, Father!'

Prayer is like a seed inside us: seedlike because it will not necessarily grow in every heart or in any sort of conditions. If we want to talk about prayer, if we want to teach it, we have rather to talk about the conditions favouring its growth. To grasp something of what prayer ought to be, we must first of all consider the two 'partners' involved: man and God. When a Christian turns to his God, he meets a God drawing near to him through the Incarnation of his Word, a God asking us questions, waiting for us and our answers. God is waiting for each of us to set out to meet him. If indeed each man's life is destined to end in a final and everlasting meeting with God, then prayer provides the way by which we proceed to this meeting. There is a wonderful harmony in the works of God. We find this at every level of existence. And because of this, the encounter with God, full, final, everlasting, waiting for each of us, can only be the fulfilment of a journey towards him begun on earth. And all genuine contemplative prayer brings with it—sooner or later—the awareness of its being the earnest of a fullness not susceptible of fulfilment here below. Anyone who has experienced—even for a split-second—this intimacy with the Lord, will know what I mean. Such prayer brings with it an immediate yearning for eternity, a longing for God never to be satisfied here on earth. These are the moments that we could wish would last forever—but in a moment they are gone. Like the apostles on Mount Tabor, we wish to tarry, to pitch our tents and stay in the radiance of eternity; but the light fades and the dark cloud of our ignorance re-engulfs our heart; we are back in daily life and Jesus is hidden once more under the commonplace appearance of people and events, visible only to the eye of faith. This full and eternal contemplation of the Lord's countenance is sometimes to be seen shining forth from men and women whose prayer has been peculiarly intense; these living witnesses are valuable to us; they quicken our longing for contemplation and the hope that feeds it.

Read for instance the meditations written by Brother Charles in this chapel. In them he gives full rein to his need to put his prayer into words, covering hundreds of scraps of paper, saying the same things over and over again; like a lover never tired of retelling his love. This was the way he prayed. He was only writing for himself. Look at the writings of Catherine of Siena, Francis of Assisi, John of the Cross, or Thérèse of the Child Jesus, where they record their experiences of the Divine Encounter. In their prayer, Christ calls them, draws them to him. In solitary prayer, St Francis is so rapt out of himself as to become identified with Christ and receive the very stigmata of the Lord. We glimpse the same intensity of prayer in Catherine of Siena and Teresa of Avila. And we could say the same of all the great contemplatives. Their prayer evinces so burning a desire to meet their beloved Lord as already to be the mysterious beginning of life eternal. In contemplation, this anticipation of the life eternal can be recognised for what it is, for a beginning, while in other respects we continue performing our transitory tasks. Living, sleeping, eating, speaking, loving, family life, career, scientific research, improving social conditions: all these activities, we know, will end. We know them to be transitory; while they drive us on. While what we are allowed to glimpse in moments of contemplation, we recognise as something that will truly last forever, something to be attained more powerfully, more utterly, in the life to come, and to be the transfiguring life of eternity. This ultimate contemplation of the presence of God, the prolongation of our prayer on earth, will transfigure us by means of the glory of Jesus fulfilled in us. Prayer is therefore essentially a waiting, full of impatient, loving longing. It cannot flourish in us, as you will easily see, unless God has revealed himself to us—dimly perhaps but none the less surely—as the Living One, as the God in Three Persons, whom we long to meet and adore. Such, in Jesus, is our divine partner in prayer.

The other partner is man. Left to himself, he seeks all sorts of things, but most of all himself. He seeks himself through all sorts of different cultures, religions, ideologies, philosophies. Through these, he tries to understand himself, to discover the purpose of life on earth and what he should do about it. Some men receive the explanatory Word by the wayside and the birds carry it away. Others are not able to understand, either because their minds are closed or because the environment is wrong: they cannot seek or imagine an ideal transcending this world and the things of this world, though their hearts be full of love and goodwill. These are upright men, but being shut up in an exclusive awareness of the visible world, do not even feel a longing for anything else. They are as though immune to the invisible. They do not know and do not understand that the seed falling on their roadside is something that has to be encouraged to sprout. Jesus knows these well-meaning men well: who have stopped short. And there are others, many others I am glad to say, who find that they do long for another life, that they do desire something more than the world has to offer them, something spiritual; what they want is the absolute, would reject anything less. This need for the absolute can be stifled, since some men are so conditioned by training and environment as no longer to admit the reality of a purely spiritual world, but the need will never stop being felt by men none the less. The need naturally is more obviously manifested in the religions of the world, particularly in the major religions: Islam, Hinduism and Buddhism. All these explore the way to the Absolute or to an Unknown God. And their followers have discovered a mysterious dimension within themselves, impelling them to explore the spiritual way. But however far they go, spurred on by love of truth, there is one threshold that they cannot cross, even when God's grace works within them. For the Word of God has been revealed in Jesus Christ, and through him alone can this Word make itself fully heard. God makes all goodwill fruitful, grace is at work, but fullness of light can only reach those who encounter the Light Incarnate. Were it otherwise, there would have been no need for the Word to come and live among us. Some men do not receive his light—why God should dispose things thus, we do not know.

Non-Christians who explore these highest paths of the spirit may indeed attain to genuinely great interior discoveries, as also to mastery of the passions. Some even reach the stage of experiencing their being as spirit, and are inspired with the hope of eventually encountering the Absolute, whether personal or not. But however advanced these mystics may be, some of them certainly being favoured with an authentic experience of the Living God, the fact remains that, without the revelation of Christ, no doctrine or religious system can normally lead the spirit of man beyond its natural limits—not even contemplation. Mystical experience, even if it succeeds in spiritualising nature, in penetrating the mystery of the spiritual ground of human life and in exploring and experiencing its remotest frontiers, can still never succeed in penetrating the mystery of Him who is altogether Other; not in achieving intimacy with Him who, more than ourselves, is the source of our being, all Truth and all Love. Only in Christ can man penetrate the secrets of the tri-une abundance of the Godhead. A man might, I suppose, gain some inkling of the mystery by the very fact of longing to penetrate it, but he could never succeed in grasping its secrets by his own spiritual efforts, be they never so lofty. Jesus alone provides access to the heart of God, for any prayer rising from the human heart. People today, reacting against a Christianity which they have more often than not themselves clumsily misinterpreted, seek the absolute in all sorts of other directions.

Supposing the quest to go beyond scientific thought but yet to be still on the same plane, they adopt spiritual disciplines from the religions of the East. Man is attracted by things he can grasp intellectually, and by techniques which he can practise in the certainty of procuring results by his own efforts.

Yet between these seekers and the Creator of all life, stands Jesus Christ, he who is the Way, the Way of prayer, the Way to the Father, the unique Bridge spanning the gulf separating the limitless mystery of God from the enquiries of men. Christ is himself the totality of life. He leads us ever towards love and this is why he can reach every man, however poor, however wretched; for Christ's love is mingled with divine compassion.

By the light of faith and the grace of Christ, our efforts at contemplation and our quest for the absolute are both made simple: more humble in approach but much deeper in effect. Contemplative prayer is within the reach of every poor and humble heart once love for Christ has taken hold of it: Christ who is at once within us and beyond all spiritual paths. Whatever path a man may choose to explore depending on his own particular mentality, and however attractive and genuine this path may be, Jesus stands beyond. You cannot capture Jesus by techniques of meditation, nor by exercises in spiritual abnegation.

Now, when God draws near to us to overwhelm us with the foretaste of what he has prepared for us by his Resurrection, 'the things that no eye has seen and no ear has heard, things beyond the mind of man', he places this God-given gift in us in the form of a seed. The seed confided to us needs very special conditions in which to germinate; it is foolish to think that it does not matter how you pray, so long as you sincerely want to do so. And here I do not mean the way prayer can and should germinate in every Christian life as the individual's state of life and generosity of spirit may determine. For prayer can germinate in the heart of a sinner, just as it can in the heart of an upright man aware of his Christian responsibilities. No, I am now talking to you personally, as having been called by the Lord to the religious state and hence to a prayer-life worthy of your dedication to the Lord's service. Prayer will be a higher and more pressing duty for you than for other people, since it is part of the Kingdom of God, for which you have forsaken all, and since it is also a leaven in the People of God to whom you have been sent; and lastly, since, in the service of the Lord, it is an essential work of the apostolate.

Some days we pray well; some days we pray less well; prayer is governed by our own poor abilities, lies at the mercy of our own limitations. The gift of God is only ever offered to us, the gift of God does not crush us, is not forced on us, but discreetly offered to us. Ours, to accept it with love.

Now I want to tell you what has to be done to the soil of the heart: we must dig it, clear the stones away, root out the smothering brambles, in preparation for the seed. Then we have to water it, to make the seed sprout. Here again we must achieve a perfect co-ordination between all that is natural in us and the action of God: for the latter never replaces our own personal efforts. If we grasp this thoroughly, we shall avoid all sorts of misconceptions. Whatever God means to accomplish in us, whatever the grace of Christ has won for us by his death, nothing can bear fruit unless the soil is suitable and unless we ourselves co-operate to the full. Whatever people may say, the 'supernatural' is a genuine, living reality. Supernatural is what we call everything God-given beyond our own possibilities, beyond the requirements of our present human condition. In spite of its divine origin, the supernatural cannot transform us unless we willingly assent, and unless there are sufficient grounds and dispositions on which it can work. There must be natural disposition, for there to be supernatural contemplation. This is why I made a point of showing that man is of his own nature seeking after the absolute when he attempts to pray. It would be a waste of time, a dead-end, if we were to try to pray without a minimum of mental, spiritual and physical preparation— Christian prayer is not like Yoga or the natural meditation of Zen Buddhism. Perfection in prayer comes from encountering the graces of Christ with a well-disposed heart and spirit. For we must want to pray and must prepare ourselves for doing so. All these attempts and efforts on our part, however, are sublimated and transfigured by the unique love of Jesus. Prayer is a heart-to-heart conversation with a beloved Being who is also our God. This is what makes Christian prayer so different. The man who in seeking Jesus has reached a condition of total renunciation (which ought to be one of the effects of religious life), will be best disposed to receive the grace to contemplate his Beloved, the One whom Brother Charles used to call his 'Beloved Brother and Lord Jesus'. How well this title sums up the nearness of Christ, who, entering our humanity, has made himself brother to each of us; and the Divine Lordship of him who is forever the author of our life! Jesus transfigured on Tabor bewilders the Apostles as being beyond their ken; Jesus resurrected evades the embrace of Mary Magdalen. The countenance of Christ, inevitably strikes us thus: near and familiar in his humanity, at the same time terribly distant in the radiance of his infinity and eternity. But this is exactly what attracts us to him, since we thirst for eternity, and the fullness of life that resides in him.

On this, the great contemplatives themselves can teach us more than any lecture can. This is why the saints have such an important place in the Church, especially the ones who have left a written record of their experiences. Suppose for a moment that we knew nothing about the great contemplatives: how sadly little we should know of what we now know about our relationship with God! We should lack what we might call a revelation in practical human terms of the intensity that Man's relationship with God can reach on earth—the fruit of Christ within him. We need this sort of testimony and adopt some of these men of God as our masters. This is how the great spiritual families have come into existence. The Carmelites have St John of the Cross and St Teresa of Avila as their daily guides in their prayer-life. Brother Charles plays the same role for us in our Fraternity. But all the saints concern us, making a great family, from one or other of whom there is always something for us to learn.

So how can we prepare ourselves for praying? Are there ways that can be taught? Certainly there are, and what holds good for you as Little Brothers or Little Sisters also holds good for those with whom you will later have to share your own experience of prayer. It is difficult to cover the whole subject of prayer, but here at least are one or two useful thoughts.

First we must be able to put everything we are into our prayer. As we only possess the present moment, we must concentrate our self-giving into that moment, so that at that moment we prefer Jesus absolutely to anything else in the world.

This is essential. We have to concentrate on the moment of prayer, so that for that brief moment at least we know that we prefer Jesus our God to anything else, to the entire creation. The disposition to accept God even for so brief a moment is not something spontaneous, but rather the product of the rest of our life. If we mean to be honest with ourselves, we have to do our utmost in the way of deprivation, to be capable in the course of our ordinary activities of preferring Jesus to everything, and of loving him more than all. Our religious life well lived should itself dispose us to prayer. If you are faithful in keeping your heart chaste as your vow requires, you will be ready to prefer union with Jesus to any human love; if your poverty is genuine, if you are attached to nothing, then you will find it easy to prefer Jesus to all earthly things; and if you serve the Lord in obedience, you will be ready to prefer the Lord to all your own activities, however useful they may be or however unselfishly directed to the good of others. Which really means that the first condition for praying is to have your heart free. This freedom varies according to the vocation you have received: it will not make the same demands on a Little Brother or Little Sister as on a religious missionary, or on a contemplative monk, or on the mother of a family, or on a layman doing an ordinary job. God does not expect the same degree of dedication to prayer from everyone, since each must be faithful to the obligations of his own state. The freedom and deprivation needed for prayer are hence relative to the obligations of the individual. A married man, for instance, will be in a proper frame of mind for prayer, if he loves his wife as he should, he will be free for prayer if, his professional and political commitments notwithstanding, he continues to prefer God and the keeping of God's law, to everything else. The availability of a heart for God is co-ordinate therefore to its duties.

For you, brothers and sisters, the genuine wholeheartedness with which you lead your life in religion is your proper preparation for prayer. In all things, have a true, pure, illusionless love for the Lord. Since however you will never feel that you have reached such a pitch of perfection as that, you must entirely identify yourselves with the state of mind of the tax-collector in St Luke's Gospel, humbly, honestly and peaceably acknowledging your sinfulness; yours will then be the privilege of meeting a merciful Lord. The tax-collector's attitude is the most truly Christian one, since only possible to someone who has experienced the breadth of God's mercy—of God coming to meet him in Christ crucified, in the heart of the Good Shepherd, content to leave the ninety-nine sheep, to run after the straying hundredth one. What a privilege to be that hundredth one! Let us not be too sure that we belong among the ninety-nine obedient, well-behaved sheep of the flock! The stray is privileged to have the Lord to itself. Odd that we should find it so hard to identify with the tax-collector! Pride? Delusion? Mistaken notions of Christian perfection? I do not know. Yet we see how immediately God's eye is drawn to the tax-collector. God's whole attention is apparently focused on him, because he is honest, simple, direct and humble-hearted. I have already said that our heart must be free and pure if we are to pray; now, our untroubled recognition of our shortcomings allows the eye of God to look deep into our heart. We must not try to hide anything from that gaze. This is the best attitude for praying.

But it is not enough for us to be humble of heart, we must be humble of mind and intellect too. The Lord's merciful love is not all that we meet in prayer; we encounter his truth. We must recognise what poor creatures we are in the eyes of the Lord, the author of our life and intellect. In many cases, especially today, our main obstacle to prayer is our intellectual independence. It is also the one most difficult to overcome. A humble heart in the presence of the Lord is not enough, for he is Truth; and God will not allow us to possess him if we are not ready to receive him as both Love and Truth. God is indeed Love, as John the Beloved Disciple testifies to us. But he is only Love because he is also Truth. That is why Jesus warns us so emphatically that, if we are to receive him, we must become like little children. In prayer, we go into the presence of Truth, we draw near to Him by whom all things have been made, to Him who has made us in his own image. To meet Him then, we must go down into ourselves until we realise what exactly it means to be a creature. This is hard. Our intellect must humble itself before the inexpressible. You see how poor this makes us— the poverty of having been created? Yes, this is hard indeed for a scientific intellect. How much must be renounced! At the moment of prayer, then, we must be totally attentive, with intellect and heart both at God's disposal. And this leads me on to mention external factors making it easier for us to be attentive.

There are certain conditions that we ought to observe if we mean to be attentive to the word of God and to make a silence within ourselves. Attentiveness, for a start, presupposes the quietening of our passions and pre-occupations: so attentiveness is one of the effects of renunciation and inner freedom. If we are poor in heart, we shall be able to prefer Jesus to all else at the moment of prayer, and this will dispose us to think only of him. I do not pretend that you will never experience distractions—these are inevitable. But we can acquire a deeper attentiveness, a waiting for the gift of God, in the heart and spirit. This attentiveness is beyond the distractions of imagination and memory and on another plane altogether.

This loving attentiveness normally requires silence. Silence is an important condition for prayer: it is hard to meet God except in silence, and contemplation may become impossible. I mean silence of course in its fullest sense, and particularly inner silence, the silence that makes outward silence meaningful. Inner silence means the silence of the heart, silence of the senses, of the imagination and indeed of the entire being in calm re-collection. We must humbly do our best to achieve this silence, not forgetting, however, that this is only a preparation for meeting the Lord, a preliminary disposition. We must not be content with that. And here lies the danger in some of the techniques of recollection. Certain disciplines can indeed impose silence on the faculties. But even if we do use these disciplines and achieve this silence, we must as it were forget about it, detach ourselves from it, since this is no more than the natural threshold to true recollectedness in God. We have to cross the threshold before we can go further: we have to consent to losing sight of ourselves.

Outward silence is also to be sought. I cannot believe that noise is compatible with contemplation. We must constantly try to set up zones of silence in our lives, since these are as necessary to our spiritual life as they are to our mental balance. Silence is a state of total listening, a sort of attempted spiritual-isation in which the body too has to take part: nerves should relax, grow calm, and we must learn to stay quiet and still while we pray: which means that we should adopt a posture allowing us to keep still. These are only remote preliminaries but none the less important, modern life causing so much tension and imbalance. Fortunately we are now beginning to rediscover how important it is for the body to play its part in spiritual activity. All inner feeling, if sincere, expresses itself through the body. Body and spirit are fundamentally linked and interdependent; thus, for example, there is no true inward respect that the body does not reflect by a respectful posture. No more is there true silence in the spirit, if the body too is not in a state of silence.

All the great contemplative orders of Christendom and all those seekers of union with God in the major religions of Judaism, Islam and Buddhism, are agreed that physical asceticism, controlled diet and fasting, are efficacious in disposing us to prayer. We do not pray well after a heavy dinner, with our body in the torpor of digestion. You remember the *Preface* for Lent, which we mentioned earlier: how it praised fasting as lightening the body and disposing it to spiritual activities. Admittedly, most people's diet today hardly lends itself to this type of restriction. The sort of fasting that I have in mind is not some impossible feat, having the effect of enfeebling the body instead of lightening it and so making us unfit to discharge our duties.

But the fact is that discipline over food and a balanced rule of life, are good for prayer, especially during retreats. We ought to think about this more often!

* * *

Among the preliminary dispositions for prayer, we have already spoken about silence. We might even say that in a sense silence includes all the rest. But there are of course different sorts of silence. There is disciplinary silence, requiring that we should refrain from talking or making a noise at certain times of day— the value of which has almost been forgotten in some communities. But reasons should in any case always be given for regulations of this sort, usually necessary for the common good, since people for instance who are studying should not be disturbed.

But this is merely a silence of convenience and can hardly be dignified with the status of a religious obligation. It has no direct bearing on the inner silence of prayer. You might call it negative silence, an absence of noises.

Religious silence is a very different thing. Its consistency and its absoluteness present us with the inevitable choice: either of entering it and inwardly accepting it, or of being frightened of it and running away. When this sort of silence is demanded of a community, it should be demanded in good earnest and should be received as a call to inner silence: a silence inviting us to go down into ourselves, there to meet God and ourselves. This is the silence in which we can discover a dimension of ourselves, a silence so deep that we can penetrate the mysteries of our own nature. By mystery I mean that man, in the way deep down he knows himself to be free, eludes scientific definition or investigation. We do not understand ourselves. And this silence brings us face to face with what we are. It puts us into a state of total listening. Deep in ourselves, it brings us into communion with the absolute Being who has brought us into existence. This silence is sacred, and it must be absolute. It is all or nothing. This is something quite different from a discipline. It is the descent into the mystery of self, and leads us to the mysterious frontier of God; it is the final preparation for listening to the Increate Word, who has called us into life by uttering our name. This you might call the silence of the desert. It takes us far away from the works of men, far beyond our own activities. Such silence would have no meaning, were the works of men the only things that are real. This absolute silence opens us to God, throws us on him, rather than suffer the ultimate hellish loneliness of imprisonment in self. Silence and solitude go together. How well the Desert Fathers understood the need for them, as we are once again discovering amid the pressures of a dehumanised society, stifling us with its mechanistic theories of what we are and how we should develop.

This is sacred silence—that is the word—since God alone gives it meaning: a zone of our existence, an interior state, where we are set apart for God. We do not have to go to the desert for this; we can find it among men too. We must arrange silent times and silent places suitable for prayer. Although we ought to learn to pray all the time and everywhere, we cannot succeed in doing this without setting certain times aside for prayer, in surroundings conducive to concentration. Since we have to purge our senses and imagination before we can establish our inner silence, the atmosphere of the place where we pray can be very helpful to us. Some places, some chapels, have the right lay-out and right atmosphere to help us empty our imagination and replace our manifold pre-occupations with an exclusive concentration on the things of God. Sacred buildings are so-called because they are intended to signify the invisible reality, and by means of things that we can see to dispose us for meeting God. Experience shows, whatever theorists may say, that the way a building is laid out, the economy of line, presence of sacred imagery, amount of light: all these factors can be conducive to recollectedness and so to bringing us into the presence of the invisible.

Here I might say a word about the relevance of nocturnal prayer. Throughout monastic history, this has been considered of great importance; as indeed it has outside Christendom too. There seems to be a peculiar harmony between prayer and the peace and silence of night. Christians go further, seeing night-prayer as a mysterious but none the less real participation in Christ's night-watch in Gethsemane. In the hours of darkness, Christ endured his agony and was arrested; night saw those terrible moments when Jesus made that agonising, unqualified act of obedience to his Father's will and freely consented to endure the passion. At night, too, he withdrew up the mountain to pray. In doing so, Jesus was responding to a spontaneous human need; we are all affected by the symbolism of night.

* * *

After discussing the right conditions and dispositions for prayer, the time has now come for us to talk about prayer itself. Prayer takes place in the encounter between the human heart and the Word of God, in a mysterious but none the less real union with the perpetual prayer of Christ. Once again I repeat what I said earlier: prayer takes place between two partners— God and man. As regards man, we have already shown that he can explore ways leading to God, even if he does not yet know how God has come down to meet him in the Incarnate Word.

In searching for God there is an apprenticeship to be served, consisting of activities within man's natural scope. But since God comes to meet us, we have another apprenticeship too, which consists in disposing ourselves to receive the gift of God when we have silenced all our active faculties. Let us call this active silence. These two elements of prayer: active quest for, and passive acceptance of, the gift of God, can never be entirely separate. They are both present in all prayer, although that prayer may take different forms. There is also an infinite variety of charisms and gifts of the Spirit. Even in making active efforts to prepare ourselves to pray, we must always be ready to receive God's visit in humility and silence of heart. Sometimes God's gift is such that it carries us beyond intermediate stages and normal procedures. We must be careful not to ignore these graces through being too much concerned with what we ourselves are doing.

The quest for contemplation may lead by many roads, often corresponding to well-established schools of spirituality, each emphasising one particular aspect of prayer. Although I do not mean to say much about this, I must emphasise the importance of the liturgy and eucharistic life in our encounter with Christ. For these are two privileged paths by which the gift of God comes to us while we are making our own efforts to progress towards him. God reveals himself to us under visible signs: liturgical rites, sacraments, the prayer of the Church and the preaching of the Word of God. Today the liturgy has recovered a pre-eminence that it should never have lost, as prime source of the prayer of the People of God. The way the liturgy is celebrated may vary, depending on the vocation of the particular community or Church. In our Fraternities, it should be celebrated with simplicity, somewhat interiorly. I do not mean this of course when celebrated for a Christian community served by the Fraternity, though even then the Fraternity's message of evangelical simplicity, as also consideration for the worshippers' sensibilities and ways of expressing themselves, should always be apparent. The prayer-life of our Fraternities should be characterised by respect for the mystery of the Divine Presence, and also by inward contemplation of it. Hence the close link between the actual celebration of the liturgy and an eucharistic life entailing adoration of the Divine

Presence in extension of the Eucharistic Sacrifice, and in union with the prayer of Christ ever interceding for us with the Father.

We must always try to strike a balance between our pursuit of the right conditions for prayer, i.e. by practising silence and solitude, by co-opting the body and by using disciplines to make our spirit attentive, on the one hand; and on the other, our pursuit of the encounter with God in simple and loving desire and poverty of means. We must never treat these two aspects of our prayer-life as contradictory. Depending on circumstances, on our personal needs, on the difficulties we experience, and on the grace of the moment, we shall sometimes put the accent on one, sometimes on the other. Thus the ways of prayer appropriate to the Fraternity can be resumed in three words: desert, Eucharist, Nazareth. The desert corresponds to our apprenticeship to prayer in times of solitude and absolute silence; the Eucharist is a constant invitation to enter into the mystery of Christ and take part in his perpetual prayer; while Nazareth obliges us to make an effort to pray continually in the midst of circumstances often difficult and apparently unfavourable. Hence our prayer needs to be nourished by the Eucharistic Presence and to be fortified by regular visits to the desert. I see this threefold rhythm as esssential to the prayer of our Fraternity and as giving it its particular quality. I might add one last characteristic: our duty to associate everyone in the world with our prayer, especially those to whom Providence or the Church's commission links us most directly. Prayer is therefore one of the hidden aspects of our work, as evangelists, thus uniting us to the prayer of Christ, the Good Shepherd.

Now, one last word about the doubts and difficulties affecting all prayer and often causing people to give up praying. We must keep reminding ourselves that prayer is the pre-eminent work of faith and hence that it shares the characteristics of faith; and that God's presence is revealed to us as much in the darkness as it is by the light. The Spirit of Christ works within us, leading us forward by the light he sheds along our road, light by which in prayer's magnificent moments he allows us a glimpse of his countenance. But perhaps in times of darkness he goes even deeper into our heart to work its transformation, when there is nothing we can do except persevere in hope. God alone sees the road by which he guides us; and by faith we put our hand in his and see with his eyes. The reason why our encounter with God in the unrelieved darkness of prayer is so painful, is that when we have reached this state we are left with no way of escape. Either we have to march on through the arid desert, by no known road, no longer seeing our destination; or we give up praying because we feel sure that we are wasting our time, or because we cannot endure the apparent futility and boredom of it, or because we wrongly imagine that the Lord has forsaken us and that prayer has therefore become useless, ineffective, and does not reveal ourselves to ourselves; it is no more use to us. Such gloomy crises of faith are not confined to prayer; they will also occur from time to time in our work. But when we are busy doing things, we can to some extent ignore the alternations of light and darkness by taking refuge in the work itself and in producing results. But then the intention informing our activities begins to change and diverge from Christ's intention, which ought to be the lodestone of every apostolate. Fleeing the darkness that God lays deep in our heart, we try to forget it by working and producing results. Apparently nothing has changed, but in fact in God's eyes everything has changed. Ordeals of faith always seem worse when we are praying and when we are alone; they are often very hard to bear.

We must constantly renew our faith in the Lord, the unifier of all life and especially of religious life; and we must do this by faithfully observing a rhythm in which action is interspersed with zones of deep silence. This is vitally necessary. And here, it seems to me that we can distinguish three degrees of silence. Silence may have been chosen as a habitual and permanent condition of life; this is what pure contemplatives choose. This silence is quite special and is the normal state in which people live who have totally dedicated themselves to union with the prayer of Christ in his Church. Then there is a silence of the same order, but temporary, which we should seek in times set apart for retreat and solitude. I do not need to labour the importance of these periods in the desert for members of our Fraternities. And finally there is that inner silence of listening for God, which is the fruit of habit acquired during our periods of solitude. This is a silence disposing us to action. More deeply, it prepares us to understand and meet other people, since the habit of silence disposes us to listen attentively to others and to put ourselves in their place, rather than to impose our own sometimes misconceived activities on them. This silence makes us avoid idle chatter, by allowing us to transcend the more superficial aspects of human relationships, in which it is all too easy to take refuge from the demands that silence makes of us. The habit of continual inner silence is a fragile one and can easily be lost if we do not frequently fortify it by times of deep silence in God's presence.

I shall digress for one moment to ask whether we are loyal enough to enter God's deep silence during our retreats. We are silent—but only more or less so. We admit a lot of noise and minor prattle. Silence of this sort may not be much good. And once again I come back to the silence that we ought constantly to preserve within us and that, far from preventing us from being completely at the disposal of other people, allows us on the contrary to be wholly attentive to them, by repressing our own tendency to talk without bothering to listen, and to respect them as they are. This sort of silence is a form of poverty, on which true charity is built.

9
The Evangelist and His Mission

EVERY TYPE OF human life has its own particular activities.
Little Brothers and Little Sisters are involved in activities—in
their work and in human relations. So what I have to say here
applies in some degree to all forms of religious life.

Religious who engage in outside activities, most particularly
of course those who have an apostolic vocation, have in the
nature of things to live in at least two environments: the community of their brothers, which is the setting of their religious
life, and the environment or environments of those whose pre-
occupations, outlook, and living and working conditions they
are on occasion called to share. A situation of this sort inevitably creates problems and a certain amount of tension. And we
may be tempted to reduce the tension between these conflicting environments by allowing one to assume primacy over
the other. From which we might arrive at the conclusion that it
would be better to secularise the religious life to a point when
it should no longer be distinguishable from the secular environment. Which means in practice, suppressing religious life altogether—since it could hardly survive without the embodiment
of its fundamental requirements in a community environment.
No, we have to reconcile ourselves to belonging to a number of
different environments, and learn to move from one to the
other, not only without ill effects to ourselves but actually
enriching ourselves each time with whatever of value each environment has to offer us. Whether we are in our community
or outside in the world, we have to remember that we are,

in either case, fulfilling the demands of our vocation. No life can develop properly without an appropriate social environment. This is why Christ founded the Church, a visible society, to be the normal and necessary environment for the full flowering of Christian life in the world. The Church provides an environment making it possible for Christians to live in the world without being of the world. And by the same token, every religious community should make it possible for religious to live among men and at the same time to be proper religious.

We must now talk about the apostolate: about its nature and about its activities, raising certain topics for consideration as we go along.

All apostolate is inevitably rooted in contemplation since the apostolate is always something done by Christ. I mean apostolate in the sense of the general mission of the Church, not of the multifarious activities more or less directly connected with it. The apostolate is the motor-power by which the Kingdom of God grows among men. Now, the Kingdom grows visibly and it also grows invisibly. Its visible growth is usually the result of the Church's apostolic labours and apparently due to organised human agency. For, after all, the various Christian communities and Churches have visible structures and spheres of influence. The invisible growth of the Kingdom, however, is the hidden result of the activity of the Spirit of God: and no one can assess the extent or depth of this. The Kingdom's invisible growth often has its source in the Christian heart, and this is the contemplative aspect of the growth of the Kingdom of God. All these visible or invisible expressions of the Church's apostolate, whether primarily of human agency, or primarily divine since invisible, are all prompted by the Holy Spirit promised by Jesus and sent by him to quicken his Body, the Church. Central to the growth of the Kingdom is the mission of the People of God, commissioned as a body by Jesus. There is more therefore in this motor-power for growth than a mere impulsion of love tending naturally to spread outwards from the centre: there is an order from Christ that has to be discharged. By virtue of this mission, no Christian has the right to refuse an apostolate which falls to him, since he belongs to Christ. So this is rather different from wanting to share some discovery which strikes us as vitally important to the destiny of mankind:

as, for instance, we might feel impelled to win other people to our own deeply-held political or ideological convictions. This imperious and often passionate need to impose our own convictions on others is one of the most powerful motives of human conduct.

The apostolate is quite different, both in source and in motor-power, from other forms of human activity however lofty, since it is an activity of the Body of Christ and since it is a divine mission. This does not stop the apostolate from being a spontaneous response to love: the apostolate should always be motivated by love, by the twofold love we bear for Jesus and for our brothers. The apostolate springs from the heart of the Lord, and this is what gives it its contemplative element, even when carried out by people who are not called to dedicate themselves habitually and exclusively to contemplation. In the People of God there is a diversity of gifts, of ministries, of charisms, of responsibilities, all contributing to the apostolic mission of the Church. I can only touch on these, but you would be wise to study them more deeply, with thoughtful reference to such conciliar documents as *Gaudium et Spes* and *Lumen Gentium*.

I have just mentioned charisms, and it is worth defining what we mean by this term, since it is so constantly used and misused today. A charism is not a natural aptitude or exceptional quality of character. It is quite wrong to say that someone has a charism for teaching, or a charism for social relationships. Why not just say aptitude or natural gift? For a charism is a gift of the Spirit freely conferred on someone for the apostolate or for the service of others. When we speak of the charism of the founder of a religious order, we mean precisely that: the man has been enlightened and strengthened by a special and habitual grace, giving him the necessary vision and power to promote a spiritual ideal and to organise a new form of religious life. The charism of the religious life, if lived whole-heartedly, ought to flower in a radiance beneficial to the whole Church. There have always been charisms in the Church and these bear witness to the way the Spirit helps the Church to accomplish her mission. The charism does indeed come to fulfil and complete a man's natural aptitudes, for some difficult task. The Holy Spirit is the sole author of a charism; a charism is not a purely human endowment, however exceptional. Another characteristic of charisms is that they are conferred for the good of the Church: for the apostolate and the extension of the Kingdom of God. You might even say that, without charisms, neither the apostolate nor the religious life could achieve true fulfilment and perfection. Although the Lord is free to bestow his charisms where he will, he usually only grants them to people whose hearts are ready to receive them. Since the purpose of a charism is the good of others or the service of the Church, it may sometimes happen that the Holy Spirit confers them on people who are imperfect and even unworthy. But this is rare. And the history of the Church is there to bear witness to the fact. Usually there is a close connection between the holiness of the people, or the perfection of the communities, and the charisms which they have received. I digress, but only to warn you against the contrary error, common enough today, of hailing activities and plans as charismatic when these are sometimes in fact far from conducive to the renewal either of religious life or of the apostolate. Now, more then ever, we need the gift of the discerning of spirits.

We must now consider the relationship between religious life and the apostolate. In *Perfectae Caritatis*, the Second Vatican Council states it very clearly: by the very fact of profession, a religious is also dedicated to the Church's apostolate in a way consistent with the mission of his own Congregation. This latter mission, as far as we are concerned, is therefore determined by the aim and spirit of the Fraternity as approved by the Church when she erected the Congregation and ratified its constitutions. Dedication, as we have already seen, implies an exclusive giving of oneself to someone or to the pursuit of certain activities. Now, the religious life automatically entails dedication to the things of the Kingdom of God, and this is an essential disposition for the apostolate. Religious dedication is total and exacting, since it directs our whole life, even its most intimate depths, towards the Kingdom of God.

Hence the obvious relationship between vowed celibacy and total dedication to the apostolate. The Apostle Paul implies as much when he says that a married man has to worry about what will please his wife, while a man who stays free for the Lord need only care for the things of God. Religious life makes us immediately and exclusively available for the things of the

Kingdom of God. Not of course that, just because we are pro-
fessed, we shall automatically be so utterly abnegated and given,
that the things of God will become the ruling passion of our life.
We have to keep examining ourselves about this and working
until we can make this care for the things of the Kingdom the
unifying principle of our life. We have to remember that we are
dedicated to a mission in the Church, at once combining our
religious life and what God expects of us in the service of the
People of God. This care for the things of the Kingdom has to
be pursued, maintained, has to absorb our activities, overrule
our personal preferences. We have to serve this ideal, this
ruling passion.

Consider how wonderfully Brother Charles of Jesus fulfilled his vocation: how patiently he worked to discover it, how
tirelessly he tried to practise it. This ruling care for the things of
the Kingdom was the unifying principle in his life, despite the
different things he had to do. For him, as for us, life had its
unpredictable turns and surprises. It had its different phases:
the desert, the invasion of his life by others, his journeys, his
intellectual labours. Despite these divergent activities, his life
retained an overriding unity: it was ruled by one great love and
dedicated to a mission, the successive demands of which he
submissively accepted. Such a life demands perfect selflessness
since the ideal, however lofty, is always only relative. That
is why any over-precise definition of the Fraternity's vocation
can tempt us into conceiving of an ideal or of a way of life as of
absolute validity, when in fact it is only relatively valid. When
I say complete selflessness, I mean that the only two absolutes
having any claim on us are God and the supreme good of our
brothers. This twofold absolute corresponds to the first two
commandments of the Divine Law, which Jesus made his own.
Everything in our life must be at love's command: love for God,
love for our brothers; everything else must be subordinate to
these two loves. Our actions must always be determined by how
best we can serve this love; not of course that we do not also
have to remain faithful to our own mission. On the contrary,
obedience to the first two commandments is what makes it
possible for us to fulfil our vocation faithfully. If someone were
to tell me that the Fraternity's mission was definable, limited
and not concerned with the absolute, that is, with what God

wants and what my brothers need, my reaction would be to say that the Fraternity was no longer offering a genuine religious life. A mission entrusted to us by the Lord should not be circumscribed and distorted by our unduly rational arguments and discussions. Everything is relative—except God and the supreme good. We must keep reminding ourselves of this and then we shall see things in their right proportions. And please do not think that in saying this I am calling the true nature of the Fraternity's mission into question—quite the reverse. And that is why I should like to remind you yet again about its basic characteristics.

First of all let me remind you—since this is the burden of what we have been saying hitherto—that the Fraternity ought to be particularly aware—with an immediate awareness constantly renewed—that its apostolic activities are grounded in contemplation. The fact that we are constantly trying to contemplate Jesus and make him the centre of our life is an essential characteristic of the Fraternity. To realise that intimacy constantly sought with Jesus is truly a characteristic of our vocation, we have only to look at the life of Brother Charles. Union with Jesus was his constant pre-occupation, expressed in a resolution which he consistently tried to observe: 'In all things, ask yourself what the Lord would have done in your place, and do that!' Although we might not be able to carry this out to the letter if we had an ordinary secular job, we can and should apply it literally in all religious and apostolic activity. Indeed, a religious, an apostle commissioned by the Church, has a duty before men and the world to be a sort of extension of the Lord and of his activities. We must have the same pre-occupations as he had, we must have the same unique pre-occupation with doing the work entrusted to him by his Father, we must learn to see the destiny of the world and the destiny of every individual as Jesus saw them. This is our unique and fundamental rule, as Brother Charles himself declares: 'This is your only rule, but the rule is absolute.'

But, you will say, a rule of life like this is no solution to our problems, for how precisely are we to know what Jesus would do in our place? And who is going to tell us? This is where loyalty comes in: loyalty to a rule, loyalty to the Fraternity and to the spirit of the Fraternity, in obedience and strict unity with our brothers. Although a rule of life is never perfect, although it only approximates to the ideal, it does none the less, broadly speaking, represent the ideal that is to be pursued, laying down a practical code of life, tested by experience and sanctioned by the wisdom of the Church as able to sustain our efforts as individuals and as a brotherhood. But none of this is a substitute for your own insight, for your own conscience illuminated by the evangelical law and by constant, intimate association in prayer with the heart of Christ. When St Paul says that we must be of the same mind as Christ so that Christ may live in us, until the stage is reached when it is no longer we who are living but he who is living in us: he is touching on a great mystery. Our conscience has to be so profoundly transformed that every judgment we make, every decision we take, shows the progressively stronger influence of our constant association in prayer with Christ. And this, in a sense, is your principal duty: that the wisdom of Christ should so dwell in you that, as with the saints, your every action bears its imprint, the characteristic imprint of his divinity. We can tell from the way some saints behaved, that they were images of Christ. You must be no less ambitious. You must not say that you are far from any such union with Jesus: it may be true, but this is what you have been called for all the same, and that should be enough to encourage you to persevere. This is what the Lord wants of you. Go as far as you can along this road: never turn aside.

Brother Charles of Jesus had a second rule of life. The words he used may sound a little old-fashioned, but the sense is modern enough. He resolved 'to see a soul to be saved in every man'. Today we may be more concerned about liberating the whole man than about the eternal salvation of his soul. And indeed, time was when man's earthly existence was accounted nothing, being only regarded as an ordeal preparing the soul for union with God after death. But we must understand what the words mean. For it is still true that man has an eternal destiny and that this cannot be fully worked out on earth. Besides, as we have already said, nothing can be final and complete on earth, as far as an individual destiny is concerned. What we have to do, even if we find it hard to understand and to put into words, is to share by the light of faith and love in Christ's own vision of human salvation. When Jesus cured the sick, he usually said: 'Go, your faith has saved you,' or 'Go away, and don't sin any more.' In these people's lives Jesus saw something else besides the transitory afflictions which he cured. May the Lord make us see as he sees! No one can be more truly human than Christ. That cannot be. Who has a heart to embrace the mercy of Christ, or the knowledge that Christ had of the human heart? Who could ever have his sensitivity, his compassion? For Jesus saw what we cannot see. But he can teach us to see and feel what we do not see. A humble search to know the heart of Jesus revealed in the Gospel. and the opening of our hearts to his Spirit, will gradually lead us to 'feel' like Jesus. This is what must be the basic rule for disciples of Brother Charles of Jesus.

Another characteristic of the vocation of the Little Brothers and Little Sisters is to meet friendship's most exacting demands in our relations with people in the world. Friendship for us in the Fraternity of the Gospel is the starting-point of all evangelisation. We draw our inspiration from Jesus's life at Nazareth.

It is as well to think what the Lord's vocation at Nazareth really means. In concrete terms, it means the life he led in that small Galilean town. But we must look further, beyond the carpenter's bench, to the underlying principle of that life. And this was none other than the love he bore for his Father, and his love for his mother Mary, for Joseph, for his fellow-townsmen and for all men. And this must be the principle for us, if we really mean to live like Jesus at Nazareth. As Jesus loved, so we must love men humbly, respectfully and however else this love may prompt us as the Fraternity's circumstances of time and place may allow. Let us be truly humble, truly little. Let us never look down on others, let our friendship transcend all differences of race or environment, wealth or poverty, culture or ignorance. This is your rule. Next, do everything this friendship may require of you, do it naturally and sincerely. The important thing when you are among men is not so much to share their material conditions—although you should do this as far as possible—but to love, as a brother, as Christ would love if he were in our place. If we lose sight of the immensity of redeeming love burning in Christ's heart and instead make outward or merely cultural conformity our chief preoccupation, we should deserve Pope Paul VI's stern rebuke, when he called this an attitude of 'sterile mimicry'. Again I say, what counts at Nazareth is Christ's heart, his feelings, his intentions: not primarily the sort of life he led. For the latter only has value as a visible sign of the invisible reality. Make no mistake: what people and particularly poor people expect from you, is not that you should live with them or like them; what they want from you is your friendship and, even more, the gift of God and the revelation of the face of Christ. To give them this, you must be genuine in what you say and in how you behave. Everything you do must be inspired by a true love for others and a desire for their true welfare, without regard to your own tastes and personal wishes. Here too, you must be absolute servants. It can happen that our desire to adapt totally to an environment and to share all its vicissitudes is not as disinterested as we like to think; there may be an element of personal gratification in the very act of adapting. Too often we forget, when we have to decide on the style of living that we should adopt, or on the methods we should use for doing things, that we ought first to consider how people are likely to react, and consult the poor whom we hope to serve.

Please do not conclude from what I have just said that I do not attach importance to sharing the conditions of the poor. What I want to stress is that outward sharing is no use unless it is the expression of a love going far beyond the more immediate implications of a particular style of life or of adaptation to any given environment.

*   *   *

This leads us to a third reflexion: we must always be perfectly genuine about what we are and what we ought to be. You must have respect for your religious personality, Little Brother, Little Sister, and not try to pass yourself off as something else. This respect is due to the gift given us by the Lord. We must respect ourselves as disciples, as apostles, as evangelists sent by the Lord. No one can take this commission away from us—for that would come to the same thing as our renouncing our vocation— any more than we can separate ourselves from the Church. By virtue of being religious, you belong to the Church, as you do by being ambassadors of Christ: your state and your mission are no less part of the mystery of the visible Church for being manifested in humility and respect for the poor. I would never claim that this sort of vocation is an easy one, least of all in some countries today. At present the Church is looking for a new image: I should say, looking for new external forms in which to make herself visible to men; naturally therefore the same will apply to our religious and apostolic life, which ought more and more to correspond with what men hope of us, with what we are in fact and before God.

We must also be content to live in a way appropriate to the message that we have to deliver; we are servants of that message, nothing more. If we are 'sent', it is because we are to deliver a message entrusted to us by the Lord. Some priests and religious today, you will find, take the attitude that they have nothing that other people do not have, and only want one thing: to live and behave in a way indistinguishable from the laity. This is over-reaction of course, though based on a legitimate desire to strip the priestly or religious state of all social privilege. Too often in the past, we priests and religious used to treat the people whom we were to evangelise as though we were superior to them; to say nothing of the difficulties of seeing beyond our own culture or civilisation, so often resulting in contempt for cultures less familiar.

We have to put ourselves above these problems if we are to practise Christ's charity to the full. For this can establish bonds of love between people who, knowing and accepting their differences, esteem each other none the less. We should be showing lack of faith in the power of love, if we were to insist on cultural and intellectual parity as a necessary first-step to unity. It is wrong, and in any case impossible, to abolish these differences: charity has the strength to unite what is different. Christ never asked everyone to be alike, but to unite in a human family transcending differences, wide as these may be. We are called to complement each other and enrich each other by our very diversity.

The apostle or the evangelist is certainly different from the people to whom he is sent, since he is charged by the Lord to deliver a message to men. We must deliver the message, we have to find ways and means of making the message heard, and we cannot default in this without betraying the Lord and his

Church. This is difficult today, we must admit. Entering the Fraternity means choosing a hard road.

In Council documents dealing with the religious life, we may here and there think we detect a somewhat facile triumphalism: the religious life is 'a glorious sign', among men, and so forth. Isn't this going rather far? It would be more accurate to say that the Church wishes and the Lord intends that religious life *should be* a glorious sign of the Kingdom, even if it is not one in fact. But even if it were, you may ask whether this would not conflict with the self-effacement, humility and abjection befitting those who are disciples of the Suffering Servant? Very likely it would! But then, men of God, when truly possessed by Christ, do not belong to themselves any more; they become, you might say, the common property of all the people who beset them, attracted by the presence of the Lord. Jesus was the humblest of men and the crowds thronged round him. And look at the Curé d'Ars, this poor priest, crushed and worn out by the crowd. Poor he was, but he became a glorious sign of Jesus his Master. When Brother Charles tells us that our vocation is to 'shout the Gospel with our whole life', he is not telling us to mutter it in secret or to live as inconspicuously as possible. He says that we should shout it; now, that is something glorious! But note what kind of glory is meant. In the Gospel the Lord speaks in similar terms: 'No one lights a lamp to put it under a tub; they put it on the lamp-stand where it shines for everyone in the house'. God has given you the gift of Christian faith; he has called you to follow him closely in the religious life, which is itself another gift. These gifts do not belong exclusively to you, but to the Church, and to everyone who comes to you. They are conferred to give light, to attract. Do not be afraid of the consequences. People will come to you? Let them come. This is why those gifts have been given you. The Lord has already warned us that 'A city built on a hill-top cannot be hidden', and he adds: 'Your light must shine in the sight of men'. This is not the light of your own personal worth, but the light of the gift you have received of believing in Jesus. We must not act as a screen; that is why we have to be little, seeing how hard it would be to be perfect! If we are poor as God wishes us to be poor, we should let the light shine through us. We must feel no false shame, no timidity, no respect for persons. We must not minimise the gift conferred, nor bury in the earth that talent received from our Master. We must not be ashamed of our Church before men. When Peter denied his Master, it was not so much Jesus he was denying as the despised group of Galileans to which Peter himself belonged. He was ashamed because people spoke contemptuously of these followers of the Lord. 'Those pathetic Galileans who had the wool pulled over their eyes . . . You were one of them, weren't you?' 'No, I wasn't,' Peter said. He did not want people to think he was one of them. Too many priests adopt the same attitude: they do not want people to think they belong to the Church. It is a problem, I know. But we must face the fact that the avowed, or unavowed, motives for this are not invariably good ones. We must be brave and loyal enough to appear to be what we are, and to be ready to be criticised or treated as madmen for the sake of Jesus and his Church. When St Paul preached the Resurrection on the Areopagus in Athens, his listeners shrugged their shoulders and went away. Fear of being laughed at, fear of being thought old-fashioned, have a paralysing effect on us sometimes. Young people love 'doing their own thing', hippies do not mind wearing ridiculous-looking gear, and being disliked by most reasonable men! Little Brothers and Little Sisters, you too must learn, not to wear preposterous clothes, but truthfully to bear witness to your love for Christ, without fear, without hesitation, without in the least concealing what you are, and without losing your way in a maze of theories about what evangelistic 'means' you should adopt. Straightforward witness to our faith is the best evangelistic method for our poor Fraternities. And we must not be afraid either of adopting a style of living and of social intercourse which is in keeping with the state of chastity especially in our spare time. We not only have to bear witness to chastity, but also to a style of living that makes chastity possible.

Another characteristic of our Fraternity is that we have been sent to the poorest of the poor and to those people who are farthest from the Church. I shall not say much about this: there is nothing very problematical here. We are well aware of being sent to the poorest of the poor, to those farthest from the Church, to those most difficult to reach, or to those who, if they are ever to encounter the Church, need her message to be presented to them in the way that our Fraternity would present it.

To carry out this mission, we have to accept the full extent of its demands—which means sharing the mainspring of our personal and fraternity life. It seems to me that Christian life cannot be reborn, let alone, deepened, in the world today, unless embodied in small-scale communities, deeply united, inspired by attentive, brotherly love and by sharing the word of Christ, where the members can help each other to live the Christian faith as it ought to be lived. Now, our Fraternities, with their particular spirituality and style of living, are just what is needed for fostering the growth of basic communities like these; and can serve as a leaven or in some cases even as a nucleus. And what is more, Fraternity experience, though not of long-standing, shows that this can be done. So this is certainly an aspect of our Fraternity mission. Experience also shows us that the function and place of our Fraternities among these lay communities, should be clearly defined. While Fraternity and lay community alike share the same ideals, the vocation of the laity is quite distinct from that of the Brothers and Sisters. The two environments should maintain their own characteristics and stay distinct. It would be wrong to dissolve the religious environment of the Fraternity, in the environment of a secular community. Let each respect the demands of the other's vocation, understanding that both are right and proper.

Now we must say something about methods of apostolate: a very complicated subject and one of special importance today, since for the first time in history all sorts of techniques and labour-saving devices are now available for the apostolate. What is our own place in all the, sometimes very complex, organisations concerned with pastoral work today? What do we mean by 'poverty of means' as being characteristic of the way the Fraternities should do their evangelising? It is difficult to give a rational definition, but it has something to do with Christ's own evangelistic methods, and partakes of the indefinable nature of the Kingdom of God which it is helping to build. Poverty of means, I need hardly say, has nothing to do with cheapness. I am talking of other values, in keeping with a way of behaving and evangelising characteristic of a heart as poor as Christ would have it poor: characteristic of the Gospel spirit. I do not think that we can give any more precise definition of how our choice of means and methods of application should reflect the spirit of the Gospel: for the choice is as varied as the circumstances and character of the individual evangelist. Be what you ought to be, and then ,you will carry out your mission as it ought to be carried out. Brother Charles simply said that Little Brothers should be 'everything they could'. Isn't that enough to go on with?

The apostolate is not the propagation of an ideal or of a doctrine; it is a testimony, in which the personality of the witness himself counts more than the methods he employs. This is the truth; and if we forget it, we shall be distorting the apostolate. Hence, any evangelistic method, any course of action, distorting the spirit of the Fraternity, or conflicting with its ideals of religious life, its poverty, its spirit of brotherly sharing, its simplicity and its humble position in society, should not be used: on peril of destroying or at least weakening this testimony without which an apostolate is no longer the apostolate. This is a general principle. Apply it as environment, circumstance and Providence may suggest.

The methods available to the modern apostolate raise problems—we could give plenty of examples—which did not exist in the days of Brother Charles of Jesus. Even so, we know how cautious he was in taking decisions in such matters: we have records of how he arrived at some of his decisions, where he notes down the pros and cons. In the Sahara at the beginning of this century, the choice of means available to him was extremely restricted. There were not many techniques to choose between. Even so, one of the things he had to decide was what sort of buildings to have. They were only built of mud in any case. Yet his Apostolic Prefect, Monsignor Guérin told him at Beni Abbès that he was building too much. He wanted to have somewhere ready to house a small community of brothers. He was still waiting for them when he died. We also have a series of reflections on the way he should travel in the Sahara, so as to safeguard poverty on the one hand and his apostolic duties on the other—since these obliged him to make long and frequent journeys. What he has to say about this shows us how aware he was of the various aspects of his vocation, with their sometimes apparently conflicting demands.

As far as we ourselves are concerned, the use of modern methods, many of them the product of technical progress, say for example the mass media, involves the apostolate in dangers that we should be wise to avoid. One risk inherent in these methods lies in the superficial way in which the Gospel message is presented to a mass-audience; whereas the fundamental qualities of life and testimony cannot usually be transmitted like this. I say danger; I do not necessarily mean incompatibility. Some modern methods can indeed transmit an authentic Gospel witness. All the same, given the Fraternity's vocation, I do not think that we should make a habit of using such methods. The simplicity of direct brotherly contact requires a different approach. The Fraternities are not called to mass-evangelism. The message entrusted to them has a contemplative dimension entailing a heightened awareness of Gospel ideals; and it is hard to transmit these ideals except by a man's personal testimony or by a community's testimony. We are heirs and guardians of a spiritual life which is true intimacy with the Lord; we cannot renounce this without renouncing our vocation. Proclaiming the Gospel must always be a witness, involving what we say and how we live. We evangelise, by first giving our life to God and to our brothers. In one of Jacques Maritain's letters, he says, writing about the vocation of a contemplative called to live in the world, that such a man's presence would only be meaningful if he became 'something usefully devourable for other people'. By which he means that the contemplative must let himself be devoured while still remaining 'usefully devourable'. While delivering his message, he must keep on absorbing it in his own life and work. Father Chevrier said something very similar about priests; they should, he said, be 'men who are eaten alive'. Little Brothers and Little Sisters should let themselves be devoured, should be eaten alive, and so, like Jesus and with Jesus, become 'the bread of life'. Our life will not provide an earthly food, but the true food of the Gospel, the very message of the word of God, and above all else Jesus himself revealed because loved beyond measure. This was what Father de Foucauld did, and this is what we his followers must do. To sum up then, the evangelistic methods that we should adopt are those that can most clearly reveal the Lord and his Gospel to the people to whom we are sent; this should be your only criterion, and the rule by which you assess your style of life and your actions.

I shall conclude with a few thoughts—too few in view of the subject's importance—on what I shall call 'evangelism and politics', or to put it another way, evangelism and building the earthly city. I use the word politics here in its widest sense, to include all activities, whether theoretical or practical, affecting the organisation of society at every level from basic units, through larger groupings, right up to international relations. And we may also include in the term, anything that encourages people to be aware of their responsibilities in this respect, or that prepares them to discharge this duty. This is a work of love, and particularly of justice.

Whatever the supernatural destiny of man, the temporal city has custody of his immediate existence. The Constitution *Gaudium et Spes* and the more recent teachings of the Church have thrown much light on this subject. All the same, we are often tempted to put a personal construction on these texts and only to pick out what happens to suit us. And so we tend to overlook aspects or refinements that the Council has put on record elsewhere. The earthly city, important as it is for man, is not an absolute; for he is called to something beyond his present existence. It is none the less true that men do have a duty to work for the well-being of the earthly city. And this lies at the root of our duty of political action: which is to keep working to improve society, to change it with a view to making it better, and to make its organisation and laws more fit to ensure justice, freedom, equity and peace for all its members: by the same token, encouraging brotherly communities to emerge in which each and every member can have the opportunity of fulfilling, as perfectly as possible, his destiny as man and Christian. This is no easy duty, therefore: the proper discharging of which is growing ever more urgent, difficult, exacting and universally necessary, since the more democratically-minded the world becomes, the more its citizens have to assume this duty with more commitment and greater sense of responsibility.

So first let us consider the true meaning of the 'liberation of man'—an expression in constant use among the warring ideologists, particularly the communists, to designate the proper aim of all political activity in the temporal city. At the same time, Christians commonly use the same expression to describe the saving work of Christ and its putting into effect by the Church and by all men of goodwill. So the liberation of man can give rise to much misunderstanding. We must think clearly if we are to avoid becoming seriously confused about the true nature of man's salvation in Jesus Christ.

The liberation of man can be regarded as something exclusively temporal, as in Marxism, where the aim is to liberate man from all the social and economic restraints inherent in capitalism. Here, the liberation of man requires an absolute revolution, since that alone could usher in a new political system from which man's exploitation by man was banished forever. Perhaps I am over-simplifying the case. However, anyone taking a realistic view of human nature can see that the liberation of man is not effected merely by changing social institutions. Man himself has to change, and free himself from all forms of egoism and from what is known as the 'bourgeois outlook'. And then again, everyone has to agree on what 'liberation' and 'liberty' are supposed to mean. No society in point of fact, not even a communist one, is free of constraint: if anything, the constraints are even worse.

Action also has to be taken to liberate man from himself. This, known in Latin America as 'conscientisation' consists in helping people to overcome their disadvantages by their own efforts: the serfdom of squalid living conditions, of ignorance, of illiteracy, and of all those other factors conducive to passivity and lack of political responsibility. People have to be made aware of their dignity as human beings, and of their ability to control their own development. This is a much more far-reaching kind of liberation, since it affects men's hearts and minds. But here again everything depends on the objective. For, according to some ideologies, the only purpose of conscientisation is to prepare for a liberation exclusively envisaged as the setting up of a new system of government by revolutionary means. So, although this work may in itself be excellent, it can, given a certain slant, be deprived of the one dimension that only liberation by Christ could confer.

For man has another dimension, the dimension of the Kingdom of God, which, as Christ said, is among us. This Kingdom is concerned with human hearts, extending its empire over these; it is never to be found in forms of organisation. The Church needs organisational forms, just as any other human institution

does, but since the Church's goal is a spiritual one, her structures are at the service of her apostolic mission in the world.
She cannot do without these structures, but they for their part
can always be challenged on practical grounds as being too
rigid, or ill-adapted, or inadequately corresponding to the
spiritual demands of the message to be delivered. But it would
be hard to imagine a true liberation of man as occurring exclusively on the external plane, even if, thanks to conscientisation, he were to shatter the complete gamut of servitude and
take charge of his own destiny, given that the only result of all
this were that he should collaborate with those who see liberation exclusively in terms of political change. What makes
liberation by Christ our Saviour different, is the way man's
heart is changed—to build a new man. This sort of change, of
which we only see the early stages on earth, is beyond the power
of man to produce and could not be the result of the best political institutions imaginable. We must never confuse the Kingdom
of God with the earthly city, intermingled though they be like
leaven in the dough—for the true task of the evangelist, of the
man sent by the Church in the name of the indwelling Christ,
consists precisely in collaborating with the grace of God to
effect this change. Man has to liberate himself from the tyranny
of his desires by following the way of the Beatitudes, by fulfilling the law of love and, finally by dying to sin and all that
leads to sin. This is a hard task, making great spiritual demands, carried out for the most part secretly and invisibly. It is
much more spectacular, and exciting, to teach the masses to
struggle and overthrow an unjust government and to strive for
better living conditions. Not that they should not strive, not that
we have not a duty to take part, but because, whatever the
virtues of the government to be set up, all this is not enough.
What sort of just society could you make with people enslaved
to their passions, unable to resist the lure of wealth, and lost to
the true sense of human dignity as revealed in Christ? What
price man's happiness and true fulfilment without the Christian
conception of love, the grandeur of it, the dignity of marriage,
the stability of the home? True awareness of these inner spiritual pre-requisites for the liberation of man is above all needed
by evangelists, by all sent by the Church, and by you, Little
Brothers and Little Sisters when you find yourselves working

with people whole-heartedly committed to liberating the poor from the slavery of an unjust society. For, if we do not at the same time offer them this deeper liberation, personal, yes, but with social repercussions—which comes about in the man redeemed, the new man in Jesus Christ—all emancipation on the social and political plane will be useless, since leaving the fundamental problem unresolved.

The way the new man regenerated in Christ behaves is, as it were, condensed and synthesised in the religious life—and this is the thought with which I should like to leave you. If the religious life is led courageously, with all its demands fulfilled, without respect for persons, without fear of appearing outwardly what in fact it is inwardly, people should be able to recognise it as the brave, strong, clear demonstration of the Beatitudes and of the effects they produce on a human life. Thus our life will be a concentrate of the Gospel, hence a leaven, with the power of communication that this implies. But while our religious life must communicate itself to men in the close bonds of friendship, it must never be allowed to dissolve; it must remain a self-perpetuating leaven. Leaven has to be mixed with the dough before it can pass on its life-giving power. But the analogy stops here. For leaven, having performed its function, melts into the mass and disappears; which must not be so with your dedicated life. The dedicated life must not be allowed to melt away. Quite the reverse: it must keep on regenerating itself to stay what it is, so that it can go on diffusing energy to all around it. The religious life must always be a concentrate of the Gospel, hard as that may be for us, criticise us as others may, or accuse us as people will of being ineffective because we are loyal to evangelical principles such as non-violence and peace. We must keep our faith so bright that we never doubt of the wonders being wrought by the Kingdom of God beyond the realm of sight. So we must stay, but still living among men, with the poorest of the poor, sharing their hopes, their struggles and their legitimate schemes for changing society. In whatever situation men are, they will always need the leaven of the Gospel, and that is what we shall bring them if we stay close to them. Everything just, true and good must evoke a sympathetic response from us. And we must be ready, when need be, to get ourselves into trouble for our friends' sake and be willing from the outset to take the consequences. All men of goodwill, all those who care about human dignity and the spiritual values on which it is based, will recognise these values in the Gospel leaven, when that is embodied forth in our own lives.

Little Brothers and Little Sisters, that is the ideal you must do your best to practise. And then, without even trying, you will be a true light lighting the paths of human progress and helping to sensitise the Christian conscience. You must be an ever-encouraging presence to all who labour for the true dignity of man. By the very fact of your religious life and the message of which it is the vehicle, you will be a guide to many. And this you must be without compromise, even if it costs you your life, in every sense. People should be able to recognise a religious as an example of the Christ-like man. This is no unattainable ideal. Let no one say that this cannot be done. It is no more impossible than Christ's resurrection and we believe in that; or the resurrection in store for us ourselves for which we hope and wait in peace and confidence. Our life forms a whole; the diverse elements are all bound together. Why should we falter just because others claim that our faith depends on some medieval myth, which distracts men from the more pressing realities of modern life. Yes, we do believe in another life, to which the resurrection is our gateway. So, let us be consistent. And let our lives be led in keeping with such hopes. For if people say this is nonsense, if they think that our view of human destiny is mythical and unrealistic, it follows that a life which only has meaning in terms of these realities, will also be regarded by them as unrealistic and futile. That is why your relationship as religious with people waging the political struggle or entirely pre-occupied with improving the temporal city, is a matter of such importance and one that you will constantly be having to reassess.

I have intentionally only touched on this subject, and some people may not think it suitable for a retreat. But our life is a whole, in which the most enlightened spiritual values keep taking flesh in situations subject to all the obligations and stresses of human life.

Appendix
The Angels and Their Place in our Life

AMONG QUESTIONS ARISING out of these talks, you have asked me about the Angels, and the place angels have in our life. First of all, then, do we have to believe in angels? This is a preliminary question we can hardly avoid, especially nowadays. Twenty years ago, a Christian would never have even thought of asking. People believed in them as a matter of course.

And we might begin by asking why people now tend not to believe in angels: which comes to the same thing as asking ourselves why we do believe in them.

Study of the Bible and the Gospel, of the content of Christian faith and of the practice of the Church over the last two thousand years leaves no room for doubting that the People and Prophets of God have always believed in the existence of the angels. Christ himself speaks of them as real beings. This much is quite plain.

I myself have always had a particular devotion to the Angels. I believe they play a very important role. Call this a personal opinion if you like, but I can assure you they have helped me to a much deeper understanding of the supernatural world.

It is worth considering the reasons now advanced for not believing in the angelic world. People say that the angels in the Bible are a borrowing from Babylonian mythology, as the names 'Cherubim' and 'Seraphim' clearly show. No one would deny Babylonian influence as regards the terms and imagery employed, but this is not reason enough. That the devotees of different religions believed in intermediate creatures of more or less spiritual nature, proves nothing either way as to the existence or non-existence of these spiritual beings, which the Bible happens to call angels. Nor do I see how you could set about proving the existence or non-existence of spiritual beings, anymore than you could say for certain that there was life on Jupiter or some distant star. Not that the comparison is a good one, since one day soon we may discover life on Jupiter, whereas the existence of angels, being of a different order, is not amenable to scientific investigation. For, if angels exist, they belong to a different world, and are of a nature that lies beyond our means to investigate. We have no scientific means by which we can establish whether purely spiritual beings exist or not. So the only way of resolving the question, as far as I can see, is by faith in teaching emanating from a divine source.

All the same, we are not as badly off as we may think as regards our ability to know such things, since one of the arguments advanced to prove that angels belong to an outmoded mythological interpretation of the universe can equally well be applied in reverse, to prove the existence of these spiritual creatures.

It is a fact that most religions and peoples have believed in intermediate beings. And the current fashion is to interpret this as being merely indicative of a particular stage in the evolution of man's knowledge of the world around him, leading him to account for natural phenomena like sun, thunder, trees and springs by imagining mysterious forces, divinities and intermediate beings.

In Islam, we find belief in angels, and also in other beings called Jinns. According to the Koran, intelligent beings are divided into three categories: men, jinns and angels. Angels, according to Islam, are purely spiritual beings, whereas jinns are intermediate ones capable of assuming more or less corporeal form. The jinns are popularly thought to concern themselves with men, to play a part in our daily life and sometimes to be able to harm us. Angels on the other hand are revered. As in Christianity, they are regarded as spiritual beings and servants of God. There are also bad angels, or demons.

So you have the same thing with beliefs in invisible spiritual beings as you have with belief in God: it is to be found almost everywhere in the world. I do not see why this universal fact should be considered a reason for the non-objectivity of the belief. It seems rather that human beings have an instinct, an obscure intuition, reaching beyond their awareness of the tangible world: even though this intuition may express itself in mythical, imperfect and somewhat childish terms.

None the less—though I cannot understand why—instead of considering what may lie behind this universal belief, people use it as an argument for denying the existence of angels. They say it is a myth! Let them prove it! On the other hand, I would myself be perfectly prepared to accept anything that historical or any other kind of research has to say about the way the imagery depicting these invisible beings has evolved, or about the names people have given them in various civilisations, or about the way one civilisation has influenced another. That the names Seraphin and Cherubim and the imagery depicting them derive from Assyria and Babylonia does not worry me in the least, and certainly does not stop the Israelites' belief in the existence of angelic creatures from having been well founded in fact.

* * *

But what, you will ask, does it matter whether we believe in angels or not? First, because it is a serious matter to refuse assent to what the Church, the Bible and the Gospel, implicitly or explicitly, continuously and certainly, teach about angelic creatures. But there is a second important reason: that the destiny of man himself differs, depending on whether or not angels exist. I shall go even further and say that the nature of man is at stake in this question of the angels.

Why does the modern scientific point of view tend to deny the existence of angels? Angels by definition are spiritual beings; whereas the modern view is to regard matter as the only reality. According to one materialistic view, human thought is a function of the brain. It does not imply existence of a spirit as distinct from matter. This is not a denial of thought, nor of intellectual life, nor indeed of spiritual life in its loftiest forms. No! But the thought-processes of man are regarded as not implying a non-material, spiritual soul able to survive after death, since that spirit is not conceived of as being real. This is the argument.

If, however, personality and self-awareness do survive after death, if in a word the soul does exist, this surely implies that incorporeal realities can exist. This is the nub of the whole thing, and this is why denying the existence of angels can have such serious consequences. The existence of man is impoverished, his very nature is diminished. You may ask why he should be impoverished. He is fine as he is; we are not denying the validity of his spiritual life, nor of his intellectual life, nor of his need for a spiritual life. To this, I reply: Man is certainly impoverished, because this argument does not admit the possibility of any survival after death.

When we say that man is made in the image of God, this is because he has within him a particle of pure spirit, from which love and knowledge proceed: for knowing and loving are attributes of the spirit. You may say: 'Are these not merely the attributes of man as we know him?' Animals are not made in God's image; man is made in God's image, in his very essence be he saint or sinner. What we mean when we say that man has been created in the image of God is that what he has within him is a true image of the life of the Trinity—of the infinite cycle of knowledge and love.

The more I study the findings of modern science, the more I believe in angels, and the more their existence seems to me rationally admissible. Why? First, because of the ladder of existence and the hierarchy of life: for I see that there is a wonderful hierarchy in living things, from the lowest degree to the highest. This hierarchy begins with plants, amoebas and elementary forms of life, rising through the more and more highly developed animals and culminates in man. And I argue: Yes, if God were like a man, that is to say, if God had a body and a loving, thinking life, then it would certainly seem natural and logical for the creation to stop at the level of the animals, to which man belongs.

Given the existence of God, do we have to suppose him an independent and purely spiritual being? That is the real question. Some people tend to accord the name God to the dynamism, the dialectic, gradually revealing itself in the evolution of the creation. We are all obliged to agree that a principle of order is evident in the creation. We cannot deny it, and in any case nobody does deny it; no scientist disputes it: the further you go, the more structures you discover, structures more complex and better organised than were ever suspected. The stronger your electronic microscope, the more infinitely minute structures can be detected. You may call this an effect of chance. It cannot be chance. Or if it is, it comes to the same thing as admitting that this order does exist, but refusing to concede that it has 'meaning'. This is what is called dialectical materialism, which consists in admitting the existence of direction in evolution, a kind of programming inherent in matter.

The question of the existence of angels raises all these problems. If people are inclined to deny their existence, the reason is that people on the whole deny the possibility of the existence of non-matter. Yet He whom we acknowledge to be God is a non-material, or we should say spiritual, being. True, in saying this we tend to argue from the negative, since we have direct knowledge of only what is material. All the same, we have intuition about spirit, being partly spirit ourselves. Man feels this quite spontaneously, all the while his intuitive faculty has not been atrophied by too exclusive an exercise of the pragmatic scientific approach. And consequently there is no civilisation on earth where this spiritual intuition does not manifest itself in one form or another. Why should God, creating the wonderful hierarchy of life observable to us, have stopped at this initial level of intelligent animal life represented by man? It would be astonishing if a Spirit-God had stopped creating at this point. And if God created man in his own image, why should he not have created even more perfect images of himself in an infinity of beings of the same spiritual order as himself?

So, the argument from evolution and the hierarchy of existence, so beautifully consistent and balanced in all its parts observable to man, if anything plays in favour of, rather than against, the existence of angels. If I deny the existence of any reality other than matter, I not only deny the possibility of the existence of angels, but also of the existence of a God independent of matter. If on the other hand I admit that a spiritual being can exist, then there is no reason why angels should not exist.

When I started studying theology, I was not particularly interested in the angels. In my childhood, I knew them through the pictures in my illustrated catechism: youths in long robes, with long, fair or dark hair and big, pointed or rounded wings. Others took the form of pouting baby-faces with much smaller wings. And I truly believed that 'Baby-Jesus' brought us our Christmas tree. Sometimes, as I peered through the keyhole into the locked room where the tree was being decorated, I thought I caught sight of wings, belonging to the angels who had carried the tree indoors, with all its stars and candles blazing.

Later, when I studied the *Summa* of St Thomas Aquinas, I was surprised to find that the treatise on the Angels was apparently almost as important as the treatise on Man. And I wondered how St Thomas could know enough about these angelic creatures, to be able to discourse at such length on their nature and their modes of knowing and acting. And I realised that what we had here was a study of the nature of spirit and that, to reach a full understanding of man, it was probably first necessary to consider the qualities of pure spirit. For this would make it easier for us to understand man, who seems to be placed between two worlds: the material, animal world and the spiritual world. Man is the join, the link, between these worlds, and this makes his position unique in creation and accounts for his internal struggles and the way he is torn first this way, then that. Man's position is in the middle. Otherwise, on the supposition that angels do not exist, man would be in a dead-end, since after death there would be nothing more to come. Whatever survived of man after death would survive in an immense void. Having left the terrestrial world, he would find no other one. And even if we concede that man does have a spiritual soul which survives after death, this would survive in a sort of non-life, a living death, such as the ancients in biblical times called Sheol. With no world of spiritual creatures to join, the surviving element of man would be trapped in a vast solitude, waiting to enter a new body through which alone it could exercise its faculties. But if indeed the angelic world does exist, with the grace and light of Christ everything is different. The human soul then enters a world of love and intelligence, enters a universe of spiritual life, in which it too can play its part. Abolishing the angels means abolishing the spiritual dimension of the universe.

There must be some form of collaboration between the two universes. And here tradition speaks of Guardian Angels. We are told that we each have an angel who watches over our earthly life. Monsieur Olier, the founder of Saint-Sulpice, had a great devotion to the angels, believing that they were delegated to every gathering of human beings: angels were deputed to watch over houses, villages: every city had its own angel. Monsieur Olier never failed to invoke them before taking any action. He may have been right. Perhaps it is so. It seems that we, as human beings, intuitively realise that we are on the edge of an immense world, peopled by intelligent, loving beings, servants of God. As men, we are on the frontier of the angelic world, but unable to cross that frontier or have direct knowledge of the purely spiritual condition.

Yes, why not believe in the world of spirits? What have people got against the angels today? What have the angels done, for people not to want them to exist any more, or to deny that they exist? I cannot help thinking that this attitude is due to their existence's being totally alien to the problems raised by atheism and materialism. The two things do not go together; are completely divorced. Belief in angels is the touchstone of a certain quality of faith; hence, people no longer believing in angels are not far off losing faith in the immortality of the soul and the reality of eternal, or spiritual, life. Agreed, we cannot picture the angels without distorting them, and without frequently producing the wrong image: but this is not what matters. What I deny is the right on historical or anthropological grounds, for scientists, for biblical critics and even for some theologians, to assert that angels do not exist. They themselves are free to believe or disbelieve as they please, but not to exceed scientifically established fact by teaching that angels are a myth no longer worthy of belief. Some people take this line with the more or less deliberate intention of stripping the corpus of Christian faith of as many elements objectionable to materialism as they can. The idea is to make Christianity more palatable and approachable for atheists. Many doctrinal aspects of Christianity offer worse stumbling-blocks than belief in the angels!

There is another difficulty too: by admitting the existence of angels, are we not also obliged to admit the existence of demons —of the angels who rebelled against God? For, like any creature with free will, an angel can sin. And belief in demons is frightening, and repugnant to modern thought. And further, the finality of the revolt of the angels against their Creator seems very hard, if not impossible, to accept. It outrages us, running counter to our notion of our own autonomy before God. We find it hard to realise that angels are by their very nature able to make a choice irrevocably affecting their own freedom, since we contrariwise know from experience that we are always in a process of development, are always in a state of instability, able to sin, able to repent, able to do wrong and able to turn again.

It may come as a surprise that there is so much to be said about the nature of angels. But the unifying principle in the various things we have been saying lies in their being derived from meditation on the nature of spirit, of love and of knowledge. Thought of in this light, these pure spirits, the angels, are seen as very great among God's creatures, with a fullness of life and intelligence, and a possibility of loving, and a capacity for contemplating God beyond our powers to imagine. What angels know, they know absolutely; and what they choose, they choose so completely that their fault, if there is one, can never be excused. When an angel sins, it sins irrevocably; it cannot turn back; such is its nature.

This then throws a little more light on the nature of these angelic and demonic beings, whose existence is undeniably affirmed by Scripture, by Christ and by the Church: as well as on the part they have played in the fall and redemption of man. Are the people who rise above immediate realities and attach importance to this angelic world, no more than dreamers?

*   *   *

In one of my earlier talks, I said that all spiritual life, to be genuine, must translate itself into real life. But this reality is not merely the material universe and the world of men. God too is real. When Christ withdrew alone up the mountain to pray to his Father, the time he spent there was not, as it were, bracketed off from his real life. He was talking to his Father, contemplating his Father; and this was much more real, in one sense, than his ordinary converse with men. Jesus was not wasting time in his solitary retreat, not even when the disciples came looking for him to tell him that the crowds were asking for him. Are the lives of contemplatives, spent in converse with the invisible world, with angels, with saints, with Christ, with the Virgin—are these lives of no use to mankind? Some people may call the lives of contemplatives artificial, an outmoded conception of what religious life should be. Yes, artificial indeed, if we were only to measure the real in terms of life on earth. Others will reply that there is nothing artificial about living in contact with another world just as real as the earthly one. Perhaps not, others will rejoin, but there is a right time for everything. First of all, a man should live his earthly life and made a success of that. The other life comes afterwards. Everyone, while alive, should do something useful for his brothers and towards improving the earthly city.

In the old *Layman's Missal* there used to be an evening prayer addressed to the Guardian Angel. Prayers like this are not used much now. Even so, angels are constantly mentioned in the revised liturgy, most particularly at the beginning of the Canon of the Mass. If there were serious doubt about the existence of the angels, the logical thing would have been to change these passages. For the *Preface* and *Sanctus* mark one of the culminating points of the liturgy, when the Church invites all the angelic powers to join their prayers with ours in the Eucharistic Sacrifice. Would it be right to make a habit of reciting or singing things that have no relation to reality? The Church has has always invoked the angels at this moment; *Preface* and *Sanctus*, where this takes place, are common to all Christian liturgies and date back to earliest times. The Byzantine rite gives even more importance to this communion with the angelic world, with its *Hymn to the Cherubim* sung at the Great Entry; while after the Consecration, the deacon used to wave a veil or, at pontifical masses, little silver-winged discs, above the chalice, to signify the presence of the angelic world at the central moment of the eucharistic liturgy. These symbolic actions may seem rather out of date and alien to modern ways of thinking, but the fact remains that they were intended to signify something real. Moses did not put statues of the Cherubim either side of the Throne of Mercy on the Ark of the Covenant, on his own initiative, but at God's command.

What we learn about the angels from the long tradition of the Church offers us a comprehensive and contemplative vision of all creation: in which man figures as weakest and least in the hierarchy of spiritual beings, yet as greatest in the hierarchy of material ones. He stands between two worlds. And this gives him his importance in the creation, making him unique. In a way therefore man is king of the creation, in that the earth belongs to him and he can at the same time penetrate the spiritual world. And the Incarnation of the Word is also at the heart of all creation. Christ, the Son of Man, is King of Angels, King of men and of the whole universe of things visible.

So what are we to think about all this? It is certainly not something to be brushed aside. Conditioning our attitude to the angels, there is always the question, whether human intellect can reach any valid conclusion about a trans-physical world, and whether it can in fact reach a state of true knowledge where this is concerned. If so, if metaphysical knowledge (i.e. knowledge that goes beyond the physical) is possible, then what we learn by faith takes on a real consistency and can be taken as true knowledge, with its own vocabulary and its own verities. If, on the other hand, metaphysical knowledge is impossible, then faith is meaningless, obscure, irrational and can only end in subjectivism. By this reasoning, any attempt to solve today's conundrum about faith's objectivity is doomed to failure from the outset.

This is where talking about angels has brought us. And inspite of all I have said about the invisible world, I doubt if I have convinced those of you who think that angels do not exist and are only mythological creatures. In that case, I can only say that this sceptical attitude is unworthy of little children entitled to inherit the Kingdom. For the angels too are part of the Kingdom. The Church, the apostles, all the saints have lived on familiar terms with the angels, and Christ knew them too. Furthermore, the Gospel drama of Cross and Redemption veils Christ's confrontation with the powers of evil, with the angels of Satan, the Prince of this world. Satan is not just a symbol or mythical personification of evil.

The mention of Satan immediately invites the accusation of dualism: which is not what any of us like. People are not prepared to admit the existence of two worlds. Man remains a mystery to the last. His integrity and self-awareness are certainly not guaranteed by denying the existence of the angelic world; whereas, if we accept its existence, man seems all the greater, all the better balanced, all the more truly himself as he grows in awareness of his dimension as a spiritual being.

I must stop here before I get carried too far. At least I hope you are now convinced that the existence of angels contributes to a better understanding of man's position in creation.